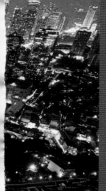

A GEEK IN INDONESIA

Discover the Land of Komodo Dragons, Balinese Healers and Dangdut Music

TIM HANNIGAN

TUTTLE Publishing

Tokyo | Rutland, Vermont | Singapore

Contents

An Archipelago of Superlatives

So let's start with the superlatives... Indonesia is the world's fourth most populous country, and its biggest Muslim-majority state. It has more than one hundred active volcanoes and something like 17,000 islands, making it the biggest archipelagic nation and the most volcanic place on the planet. It is home to more than a quarter of a billion people, but most of them live on Java which is about the same size as Illinois and is therefore, somewhat predictably, the most densely populated island on earth. The distance between Indonesia's westernmost and easternmost extremities is about the same as that between London and Tehran. Indonesia is also Southeast Asia's biggest economy, and the world's third largest democracy.

And that's usually about as far as anyone gets. It's almost as if Indonesia is just too big to make sense of; the safest option has long been to ignore it. For many years, when I mentioned Indonesia to people—be they Brits, Americans, or Indians—all too often they'd respond as if I was talking about a miniscule banana republic. Either that, or they'd enthuse about Bali, as if that was all there was to Indonesia. And on the rare occasions when Indonesia made it into the international headlines, the news was almost always bad.

But in the last few years things have started to change. First up, in 2013 the influential economist Jim O'Neill decided that Indonesia was a "MINT", one of the emerging nations likely to be the economic superpowers of the 21st century (along with Mexico, Nigeria, and Turkey, plus an earlier acronym-making quartet, the BRICs of Brazil, Russia, India, and China). Stock newsreel footage started showing gleaming Jakarta skyscrapers instead of smoking volcanoes, and alongside stories of

Top Left *Macet*—the Indonesian word for gridlock—is an unavoidable fact of life in the nation's cities.

Above The *becak* is the Indonesian incarnation of the pedicab.

Left The tourist brochure version of Indonesia does still exist, in the rice terraces of Bali and in plenty of other places besides!

Photo! Photo! Village kids in Sumatra jostle for center-stage whenever a foreigner happens to pass by with a camera.

Hello Mister!—My Personal Journey

I must have been about seven years old when we did the project about Indonesia at school. Why the teacher thought that a tropical country 7,000 miles (11,300 kilometers) away might be of relevance to a bunch of kids from a little mining village on the brink of the North Atlantic, I'll never know, but I do remember learning about buffaloes pulling ploughs in paddy fields. I went home, dug a trench in the yard, filled it with water, and threw in a handful of my mum's pudding rice. It didn't grow. And neither, to be honest, did the idea of Indonesia.

But fast-forward to the middle of my second decade, and Indonesia was looming large in my imagination. Like many teenagers from Cornwall, I was a fanatical surfer, and on chilly onshore days I'd lie on my bed poring over the cobalt-blue pages of surf magazines. I'd still have struggled to pinpoint Indonesia on the map, but I knew the names of its fabled surf breaks by heart—Uluwatu, Padang-Padang, G-Land, Desert Point.

A few years later, and my peers who had spent summers saving their pennies working on farms or in restaurant kitchens started disappearing eastwards

for months each winter. Indonesia, they said, was the cheapest place on the planet to score good waves in warm water. They generally didn't bring home any souvenirs, but one friend, Stefan, did buy something in Indonesia. It was a cassette tape. We had a shared love of American punk rock, and he handed it to me saying, "It sounds a bit like NOFX." It was the second album from the Balinese punk band Superman is Dead, and Stefan was right: they did sound a bit like NOFX.

By the time I'd saved enough of my own pennies to head for Indonesia myself—winging my way to Bali through the monsoon thunderheads in the immediate aftermath of the 2002 Bali Bomb—I had a peculiar image of the place. I was expecting to find surf,

The wide blue yonder: exploring a remote corner of Indonesia by motorbike and backpack.

paddy fields, and punk rock. I found all of them, and a lot more besides.

I've been in and out of Indonesia for a decade and a half now, sometimes wandering the outer reaches of the archipelago as a backpacker; sometimes living and working for extended periods closer to the heart of the country as an English teacher and a journalist, and I've still got a geeky enthusiasm for all things Indonesian. There's a past and a present that are equally colorful. There's a music scene that might just be the most multifaceted in the universe. There's food that'll have you scurrying for second helpings (or, occasionally, recoiling in terror!). There are mountains to climb, football hooligans to dodge, urban chic to admire, and always a new journey to be plotted— these days usually with a whole legion of hip local travel bloggers to give you inspiration.

But the single best thing about Indonesia is just how much Indonesian people like to talk. It's always dangerous to make sweeping generalizations about any country, let alone one this big, but I can safely say that talking is one thing that unites Indonesians—whether they're smartphone-toting mallrats in Jakarta, or villagers in the wilds of Nusa Tenggara. Wherever I'm wandering, when locals lounging in some roadside *warung* shout "Hello mister!"—the standard greeting for a passing foreigner—if I pause to chat, once they've stopped laughing at the concept of a *bule* ("whitey") speaking Indonesian with a (sort of) East Java accent, I'll often find myself still there two hours later, still shooting the breeze. And when the topic is Indonesia itself, there's always plenty to talk about...

Above In places like Kupang, West Timor, public transport comes with a punky style and a bass-heavy sound system blaring the latest hits.

Above right One of the unifying elements of Indonesia is a passion for flavorful street food, on offer in lively night markets and roadside stalls.

astronomical economic potential came tales of mind-boggling social media usage. An edgy Indonesian novelist got flavor-of-the-month status with New York literati; a Welsh film director made Indonesian martial arts the coolest thing on the planet for violence-loving movie geeks; and Internet news feeds started pointing out that the country's president was a hard-rocking Metallica fan. Oh, and Agnes Monica, Indone-

Left Modern Jakarta—known by many foreigners but few locals as "the Big Durian"—is one of Asia's biggest and most frenetic cities, a place with a constant construction boom and similarly constant traffic problems.

sia's favorite child star turned pop princess, recorded a single with Timbaland. Seriously. There was still plenty of bad news about natural and manmade disasters, but it suddenly seemed that the people affected were as likely to be urban hipsters as rice farmers.

But if it's no longer possible to totally ignore Indonesia, it can still be very difficult to make sense of it. Tourist guide-

Right Part kitsch, part cool—a classic Indonesian combination—finds colorful expression in these vintage bikes for hire in Jakarta's Fatahillah Square, complete with pink colonial pith helmet.

Indonesia

N

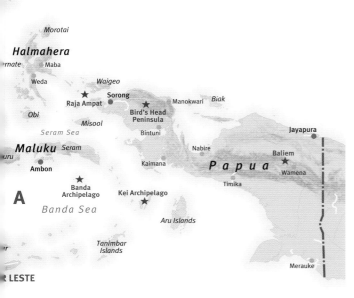

Morotai
Halmahera
rnate   Maba
Weda   Waigeo
        ★ Sorong
Raja Ampat   Manokwari Biak
Obi   Bird's Head
   Misool   Peninsula
Seram Sea   Bintuni
Maluku Seram   Jayapura
uru   Nabire
Ambon   Baliem
         Kaimana   P a p u a   ★
         ★   Wamena
A   Banda   Kei Archipelago   Timika
    Archipelago ★
Banda Sea
         Aru Islands

      Tanimbar
      Islands

r LESTE   Merauke

books still paint it as a place of temples, rice terraces, and timeless tradition, in wild contrast to the journalists poring over the latest growth figures, or bemoaning environmental catastrophes. The country's status as one of the most successful democracies in Asia doesn't sit easily with bad memories of violence and political turmoil, and the idea that it's "the world's biggest Muslim country" can be very confusing when you take into account lurid stories of celebrity scandals. And Agnes Monica's Timbaland collaboration is about a million miles away from the plaintive tones of a gamelan orchestra.

This book is an introduction to what Indonesia has on offer for travelers—its beaches, its mountains, its traditions. But it's also about the space between the hard news stories and the soft guidebook images where millions of Indonesians lead their lives, a paradise for foodies, surfers, and punks, and a country with 700 indigenous languages and 30 million Twitter users. With any luck it might just convince you that Indonesia deserves to add another superlative to its already impressive roster: the coolest country on the planet...

CHAPTER 1

INDONESIA TODAY

A social media-mad nation where old ideas of status and respect still run deep, where easygoing welcomes offset fierce national pride, and where everyone from Sabang to Merauke speaks a single language—which might not be quite as easy to learn as you've been told, and which has a youth-speak version that'll make your head spin. Indonesia today is a frenetic, and at times contradictory, place with an energy all of its own.

INDONESIA IN A SNAPSHOT

It's a very long way from one end of Indonesia to the other—3,274 miles (5,269 kilometers), in fact. The space between those far-flung points is filled with a magnificent chaos of islands—approximately 17,508 of them, but who's counting? Seriously, who actually is counting? Previous estimates of Indonesia's island tally have ranged from a mere 13,667 all the way up to 18,307. What matters more than any precise number of islands is the staggering diversity of human experience that's going on, right now, within this vast archipelago. Indonesia is home to something like 255,462,000 people, but once again, who's counting? (Actually it's Indonesia's Central Bureau of Statistics in this case). Scattered across that 3,274-mile, 17,508-island space, they range from Internet entrepreneurs to subsistence farmers, from classical musicians to supermodels, and from LBGT activists to religious evangelists, all living out myriad lives to a soundtrack that spans the gamut from *dangdut* to death metal.

FROM SABANG TO MERAUKE

Start at the top: drifting off the northernmost tip of Sumatra you'll find a ragged little scrap of land by the name of Pulau Weh. Its main town, Sabang, is one of the proverbial poles of the nation. When Indonesians want to invoke the entirety of their supersize homeland they say "from Sabang to Merauke" (Merauke is a small eastern city close to the border with Papua New Guinea). It's a bit like when Brits say "from Land's End to John O'Groats"—except that there's no way in the world you could cycle from Sabang to Merauke in 48 hours…

Pulau Weh is the perfect image of a tropical island, and right at this very moment, in one of the guesthouses back from the beach in the village of Iboih, there's bound to be a gang of hip twenty-somethings from a big Indonesian city, chilling out after their latest dive excursion, and doing their best not to think about heading back to school or the office next week. And see the one with the laptop? She's working on a post about this trip for her travel blog.

Swing up, out, and southeast down the length of Sumatra with its cities shining like bright constellations in a great green emptiness. In Medan there's a mob of teens queuing for the cinema in the glitzy Sun Plaza shopping mall, and down across the equator in Palembang there's a couple on a first date in a floating restaurant on the banks of the River Musi. Head on southwards, across the Sunda Strait to Java, and before long you'll see a smoky smudge up ahead, with a forest of slender skyscrapers rising into clearer air. It's Jakarta, a massive maelstrom of energy raging above a sludgy tide of traffic. The richest and the poorest, the most radical and the most conservative, and people from every corner of the country and many corners of the globe—they're all here, and most of them are stuck in that traffic. In a TV studio in the west of the city, a short way off the Jakarta-Tangerang toll road, there's a glamorous

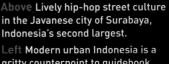

Above Lively hip-hop street culture in the Javanese city of Surabaya, Indonesia's second largest.

Left Modern urban Indonesia is a gritty counterpoint to guidebook images of timeless rural traditions.

Far left Indonesia's national flag, *Sang Merah-Putih* ("The Red and White"), is a potent emblem, closely associated with the country's bloody struggle for independence from the Netherlands in the 1940s.

Left Another world: in the hugger-mugger mayhem of the big cities, it's easy to forget that much of Indonesia still *does* look just like those glossy guidebook images—a world of forests, mountains and rice terraces, like these in East Java.

celebrity waiting in the green room of a daytime chat show, and back in the center of town, on the fifteenth floor of a high-rise office block, an intern in an advertising agency is sucking at a cup of take-out coffee and sneaking a look at a blogpost about Pulau Weh he just saw linked on Facebook…

HEADING EAST
Up over the mountains to Bandung, where, in a garage in a northern suburb, there are four skinny kids with electric guitars who, though they don't know it yet, are going to win an MTV Asia award in 18 months' time. Onwards, eastwards, weaving in and out of the looming volcanoes that run the length of Java, the sprawl of red-tiled roofs that makes up Yogyakarta appears below. The heart of the city is an old royal palace, still home to a reigning sultan and still governed by ancient protocol. But a little way north, on a busy street near the Gajah Mada University campus, a gang of students are planning an anti-corruption demonstration over bowls of noodle soup—although one of them is a bit distracted by something about Pulau Weh that he's reading on his iPhone…

In Surabaya the members of a vintage motorcycle club are planning a weekend road trip to the mountains, and in Banyuwangi a group of absurdly talented buskers are singing their hearts out for coins on a Bali-bound bus. Across the next narrow stretch of water, in Bali itself, a trio of thirty-something professional women from the capital are on a shopping spree in Seminyak,

while a few streets away a local family with a property portfolio worth millions of dollars are getting dressed up for a major Hindu ceremony. On Lombok student mountaineers are posing for selfies, 12,224 feet (3,726 meters) up on the summit of Gunung Rinjani. Back down at sea level, and one island further east, a ten-year-old village boy with a hand-me-down surfboard left behind by a traveling Australian is paddling out for his daily after-school session in the waves, completely unaware that in a decade's time he'll be competing on the World Surf League Men's Tour.

Indonesia sprawls away to the north and the east, with a hundred passenger jets streaking contrails in all directions. In the middle of Kalimantan there's a

trucker with a load of timber, cramming Iwan Fals into the cassette deck and settling in for the long-haul, and in Makassar a middle-aged woman with a small empire of takeaway food stalls is heading for the Trans Studio Mall with the grandkids. In Ambon some young entrepreneurs are frantically plugging their new alternative clothing distro store on social media, and in a village of thatched houses in the green hills of Flores a ten-year-old in a red-and-white school uniform is trying to download an Agnes Monica song on a weak Internet connection.

And still further east, in the terminal of Merauke's modest airport, an environmental scientist on his way home to Jakarta after a site visit, is hunched over his iPad scrolling through a pithy description of a far-off island on a travel blog. He reaches for his phone and thumbs a message to his girlfriend—"Next trip, we're going to Pulau Weh…"

There's a theory—a serious one—that Jakarta's addiction to social media is fueled by the amount of time its residents spend thumbing their smartphones while stuck in traffic!

A LAID-BACK NATION WHERE "FACE" AND RESPECT ARE EVERYTHING

One of my earliest impressions when I first arrived in Indonesia was of a sense of casual informality. This, it seemed, was a gloriously laid-back sort of country where people were perfectly at ease in one another's company and untroubled by crippling social niceties. The average Indonesian scene certainly made a refreshing contrast to a roomful of socially awkward Englishmen, brash Australians or Americans, or conformity-bound Japanese. And on the surface, Indonesian society usually does seem decidedly easy-going. But make no mistake, there are powerful forces at play beneath the surface.

National pride, humor and creativity: when a number of foreign governments issued security warnings about travel to Indonesia in the early 2000s, someone came up with a wry response that has since become a popular tee shirt and bumper sticker.

Of course, in a place this vast and this diverse you won't get very far trying to identify universal societal norms. A middle class Muslim from a big city in the north of Sumatra is never going to have the same ideas about what makes up normal social behavior as a poor Christian from a remote village in Maluku. But there *are* a few things that you can generalize about. One is the unavoidable influence of *gengsi*, and another is the admirable emphasis placed on respect…

KEEPING UP APPEARANCES
One of the most powerful social forces in Indonesia is a thing known as gengsi. It gobbles up huge chunks of Indonesian salaries each month; it prompts untold anxieties in the hearts of young and old; and it has manufacturers of new smartphone technology rubbing their

You Scratch My Back...

You'll often hear talk in Indonesia of a concept called *gotong-royong*. It means something along the lines of "communal effort", and people sometimes proclaim it the ultimate example of selfless community spirit, part of a supposed Indonesian tradition of folks getting together to get something done for the good of all. All very nice, but those who observe *gotong-royong* in action find that the truth is a little more complicated.

The classic example of *gotong-royong* is the way entire villages would traditionally pitch in with donations in cash and kind to allow an individual family to hold a lavish wedding ceremony. But these donations were never meant to be gifts, pure and simple; they came with strings attached. Careful note of who'd given what would be taken on both sides, and a like-for-like repayment would be expected when it was time for another family in the village to hold their own wedding feast. The same sort of careful accounting applied even when the "donations" were only of time or labor. Far from being all about selfless communal action, *gotong-royong* in its traditional form is really a system designed to bind a community together in a web of debts and credits.

Balinese women get together *gotong-royong*-style to tackle preparations for a traditional ceremony.

From East Nusa Tenggara (**top**) to Jakarta (**middle**) Indonesians are seriously sociable people.

Right Football and friendship— young fans of the Persebaya soccer team hanging out on the streets of Surabaya.

hands with glee. Gengsi is usually translated as "face", or "prestige". Basically, it amounts to the idea that if you've got it, flaunt it—or if you haven't got it, buy it on credit and flaunt it anyway.

The urge to ostentatiously display your wealth is by no means unique to Indonesia, but it does seem to have a particular potency here. It drives choice of schools and universities. It has an impact on where people choose to shop, eat, and holiday. And it definitely affects domestic architecture. When I first moved to Surabaya, the capital of

East Java and Indonesia's second largest city, I lived in a middle class suburb, close to the most prestigious shopping mall in town. The quiet inner streets of each block were lined with modest bungalows, but the much less peaceful outer lots, facing directly onto the busy traffic, were taken up by some of the most flamboyant private homes I've ever seen. Their owners had deliberately chosen to build in these noisier, less private positions because they *wanted* as many people as possible to see their gargantuan concrete and marble concoc-

tions, complete with Doric columns and statues of Greek goddesses. That's gengsi in action.

Of course, not everyone can afford to build a Greco-Roman extravaganza at a prime roadside location, but gengsi impacts consumer choices across society, not least when it comes to those two Indonesian essentials: the motorbike and the mobile phone. The pressure to have the latest, most *keren* ("cool") model is huge, even if the price tag is way beyond your means, and this is where I think gengsi has its most negative impact. Phones (the Blackberry used to be *the* phone to have; these days it's the iPhone) and motorbikes are routinely sold on credit, and there are many millions of people on very modest incomes making monthly payments they can ill afford for something that will no longer be at all *keren* by the time the debt is paid off.

The funny thing is, if you ask almost any Indonesian about gengsi they will insist that it's a bad thing. They'll make a clear distinction between gengsi and the much more positive idea of *harga diri*—"self-worth", or "dignity". And someone who is obviously a slave to gengsi beyond their means will probably

ALAY: The *Way* Too Much Kids

Of all the myriad trends that Indonesia's seething cities have thrown up in recent years, none has matched the impact of the wacky, cartoonish, and downright ridiculous cultural phenomenon known as *Alay*. No one really knows where the term originated. Some claim it's an abbreviation of *anak layangan* ("kite kid") after the traditional young kite-flyers of working class neighborhoods, but personally I think it's more likely to be short for *anak lebay*, which means something like "*way* too much, kid"!

So what exactly is an *Alayer*, and why do those Indonesians who consider themselves sophisticated look down on them? The closest English-language equivalents I've ever been able to come up with are "try-hard" and "wannabe". Imagine some wannabe Paris Hilton and her wannabe gangster-rapper boyfriend from Hicksville, Nowhere—that would be kind of Alay. But Alay culture also has some very specific features, inextricably linked to social media.

Have you ever posed for a selfie in front of a famous tourist attraction, trying to get the cutest 45-degree angle possible while at the same time pouting provocatively and putting a finger to your lips? And have you then used your phone's built-in image editing tech to add pink stars plus your name in sparkly lettering before posting the thing on Instagram? And have you ever written a text message L1k3 7h15? If the answer's yes, then you're totally Alay, and any true Indonesian hipster worth his skinny jeans hates you!

The term Alay first went mainstream sometime around 2011, and it was mainly used in a pejorative sense. Alayers were roundly mocked as being not only wildly narcissistic and entirely lacking in taste, but also probably pretty kampungan, which gave a nasty edge of class snobbery to the whole thing. There were even serious campaigns to immediately unfollow or unfriend anyone you spotted using 4L4y 5tyL3 writing on social media. Exactly what prompted this anti-Alay outburst is hard to explain, but the best theory I've heard is that it was a moment of embarrassed reflection on the part of Indonesia's first generation of digital natives—there was some kind of collective realization that for the past social media-dominated decade they'd all been behaving, well, kind of Alay, and that it was now time to grow up.

But Alay just won't die. These days there are those who embrace the term—proud Alayers, no less. And even the digital hipsters aren't beyond posting the occasional Alay selfie, usually with an #Alay hashtag—just to show that they're being ironic, of course...

be mocked as *sok kaya*—"pretend rich". But almost everyone feels its insidious pull, because if you don't happen to have the latest phone and motorbike there's always the terrible prospect of being seen as *kampungan*—literally "villagey", but meaning something close to "hick" in the American sense or "bumpkin" in Britain, also known as *ndeso* in Javanese. And whether they'll admit it or not, most people would much rather risk being judged as *sok kaya* than kampungan!

SHOW SOME RESPECT!

If the debt-inducing draw of gengsi is often a negative factor, a much more positive Indonesian universal is the value given to respect, and the idea of "softness" in interactions between people. Deep respect for your elders and superiors; avoidance of any dramatic displays of emotion, especially anger; and general politeness when talking to others: these things run deep, wherever you are in Indonesia. But if that all sounds like a recipe for stiff upper lips and starchy formality, that's not the way it works at all. In fact, it's precisely what underpins the easy-going social warmth of Indonesia. The emphasis is on being at ease, and making sure that others are at ease, and being polite and avoiding emotional outbursts are a big part of that.

The subtlety of this stuff can, naturally, make it hard for foreigners to spot it in action—and equally hard to spot transgressions. On a number of occasions I've been out and about with an Indonesian friend, and I've slowly become aware that they are angry about something. When I ask what's up, it turns out it's all down to some tiny deficit of politeness on the part of the

Military order gives way to easygoing informality amongst these soldiers enjoying some downtime during a disaster relief operation in Sumatra.

waiter in a restaurant we left 20 minutes ago, or the ever-so-slightly disrespectful tone of the checkout girl in the convenience store we dropped into for phone credit—things of which I, bumbling foreigner that I am, was entirely unaware.

Inevitably, it's also very easy for bumbling foreigners to make transgressions themselves, without ever realizing it. For example, standing with your arms folded or your hands on your hips (both poses which, unfortunately, come naturally to me) looks not just arrogant, but also downright aggressive in an Indonesian context. And getting worked up, shouting, and flapping your arms about—even if you've got an entirely legitimate reason to be angry—will get you absolutely nowhere.

It's probably true to say that in modern urban Indonesia the traditional importance of respect and restraint are giving way a little. Waiters and checkout girls are getting a bit ruder, as they are in big cities the world over, and you do sometimes see couples arguing noisily in public. But it'll be a long time before the value of respect and restraint fades away entirely.

Indonesia's national emblem is the Garuda—an eagle-like creature from Hindu mythology. It is the embodiment of Pancasila, the national ideology. *Bhinneka Tunggal Ika*, the Old Javanese phrase on the scroll that the Garuda grips in its claws, is the national motto, literally meaning "different but one", and usually translated as "unity in diversity".

Is Indonesia a "Muslim Country"?

Whenever I spot the phrase "the world's biggest Muslim country"—or worse yet, "the world's biggest Islamic country"—in a news report about Indonesia I growl and reach for my imaginary copy editor's pen. To my pedantic mind the correct description should be "the world's biggest Muslim-majority country", because that's precisely what Indonesia is. "Muslim country" or "Islamic country" suggests somewhere like Iran or Pakistan where Islam is enshrined

Inside the Istiqlal Mosque in Jakarta, Indonesia's biggest place of Muslim worship.

as a state ideology, and where the religion is the dominant decider of social values. But Indonesia's just not like that.

If you've ever spent time in other Muslim-majority countries—from Morocco to Bangladesh—you'll sense a subtle difference as soon as you arrive. It's not simply that Indonesia is markedly more liberal (although it is generally much more liberal when it comes to the position of women, and social values around boyfriend-girlfriend relationships, for example, than anywhere in the Middle East). There's also the impression that Islam is not what sets the universal tone of daily life here. Sure, there are mosques and people in obviously "Muslim" dress—and in recent years an increasingly noisy and politically influential Islamist fringe, which some fear is beginning to change Indonesia's long-famed diversity and tolerance for the worse—but in most big cities there are also bars and girls in short skirts.

Islam is just one of six officially recognized national religions in Indonesia, and though it accounts for by far the biggest chunk of the population (something like 85 percent) there are big swaths in the east of the country which are Christian-majority (plus Bali, where most people are Hindu). And religious minorities tend to be disproportionally represented in major urban populations, as well as being disproportionally represented in the ranks of the middle classes, which gives a certain cosmopolitanism to the modern urban scene. But there's also a vast diversity within the Muslim population itself—from those who take their faith very seriously indeed, to those for whom it's nothing more than a word on their identity card. There is a minority of women who adopt conservative Muslim dress, but they're massively outnumbered by those who match a simple headscarf with skinny jeans, or who wander around in shorts and tee-shirt with their head uncovered.

There are some regions of Indonesia where the local culture is more obviously and conservatively Muslim—the north of Sumatra, for example. But despite a definite conservative trend of late, when it comes to lifestyle and social norms, Indonesia is still often closer to the Buddhist-majority countries of mainland Southeast Asia than to the Middle East. So the next time you spot the phrase "the biggest Muslim country in the world", reach for your red pen...

RELATIONS WITH THE OUTSIDE WORLD

Here's the weird thing: almost everyone who visits Indonesia comes away with the impression that it's one of the friendliest places on the planet; but this ultra-hospitable nation also has a long tradition of prickly relationships with its neighbors and lapses into xenophobic nationalism. It's probably all down to history. During Indonesia's early decades of independence from the Netherlands, the flamboyant first president, Sukarno, realized that one of the best ways to bind a vast and diverse nation together was to start a fight with someone else. He started fights with America, with Britain, and above all with Malaysia.

Those days of open confrontation are long gone, but the legacy remains. Nothing starts an Indonesian Twitter-storm more quickly than a perceived insult from a foreign nation. Malaysia, which has a lot in cultural common with Indonesia, comes in for a particularly large amount of flak, and relations with the other big neighbor, Australia, can get pretty testy at times too—over everything from the history of East Timor to the export of beef. None of this ever seems to impact on how most Indonesians respond to individual foreigners, which is refreshing, but that doesn't mean that race isn't an issue in Indonesia…

IS INDONESIA RACIST?

Some grumpy expats—and boy, can some expats be grumpy!—like to claim that "Indonesia is the most racist country on earth". To my mind this is total hyperbole, and stems mostly from the fact that for the average Caucasian Westerner, living in Indonesia offers a first experience of routinely being viewed in terms of skin color—not something that any African-American or British Asian would find particularly unusual.

But if Indonesia isn't the most racist country on earth, it's certainly a place where the idea of "political correctness" hasn't yet had much impact. Caucasians are routinely referred to using the slang racial designation *bule*, and people merrily make comments about the "frizzy hair" of Africans and the "slitty eyes" of Northeast Asians. There's also a high degree of color-consciousness. As in many other Asian countries—as, indeed, in just about *every* country until comparatively recently—there's an insidious connection between skin color and social status. Basically, if you've got darker skin it suggests that you're poor. In Indonesia having a suntan doesn't mean that you've just been on holiday; it suggests you've just been working in the fields.

Indonesia also has plenty of internal ethnic prejudices. People from the far east of the country, where dark-skinned, curly-haired Melanesian ethnicities dominate, are often subjected to condescending prejudice in western Indonesia, and the famously hard-working economic migrants from the island of Madura are routinely slandered as violent, foul-mouthed thugs—much as Irish migrant laborers were once viewed in Britain.

The single biggest racial issue in Indonesia, however, centers on the Chinese. Indonesia has been home to significant numbers of people of Chinese origin for centuries—and for centuries Chinese-Indonesians have been subjected to prejudice and sporadic hostility. Under the Suharto government during the last three decades of the 20th century, Chinese language, script, and cultural celebrations were officially banned, and Chinese-Indonesians were pushed to adopt "Indonesian"-sounding names.

There's no getting away from the uncomfortable fact that, even today, Chinese-Indonesians are a disproportionately wealthy group compared to

Two versions of the intercultural encounter: Local kids watching with amusement as a tourist "roasts" herself on a Lombok beach (**left**) and an Australian trainee teacher lending a hand in an Indonesian classroom (**below**).

Is "Bule" a Racist Word?

If you're a Caucasian foreigner and you spend any time in Indonesia you'll hear it: bule. It's just two simple syllables (the pronunciation is "boo-lay"), but it's a word powerfully primed for controversy. Bule originally meant "albino", but in its modern colloquial sense it's generally used for Caucasian foreigners. As far as I'm concerned the most accurate translation is simply "whitey". So bule is unquestionably a racial designation, and some Caucasian expats get very upset by it. But is it actually a racist word?

Very few Indonesians are even aware of the idea that bule might be a contentious term. And if they do hear expats complaining they are usually defensive: "We don't use it as an insult," they protest; "It's just a word for white people!" The response to this from those determined to be offended is that in 1900s Mississippi, in its average daily usage, the "N-word" wasn't consciously used as an insult either; it was "just a word for black people".

For what it's worth, my personal take is that bule is not, of itself, a racist word. It's almost never used with insulting intent. If Indonesia had a higher degree of "political correctness", then it might justifiably be judged as problematic, but for the moment being called bule doesn't bother me one bit, and I use the word myself. It all comes down to the fact that to be happy as a foreigner living or traveling in Indonesia, you need to remember that you *are* a foreigner, that you do look different. Keeping this all in perspective can be hard if you spend your time in tourist or expat hotspots. But I know that when I'm riding my motorbike through the hinterlands of Java and I spot another incongruous foreigner, even I find myself staring. In fact, I sometimes have to fight the urge to shout out as I pass — "Hello mister! Hello bule!"

Protesters in Jakarta getting hot and bothered over an international trade agreement.

THE OTHER SIDE: IDEAS ABOUT BULES

Some prejudices are just downright funny. The one that makes me laugh most comes in the form of a common question: "Tim, why do you bule guys prefer black girls?" When Indonesians say "black" here, they don't mean people of African heritage; they mean Indonesian girls with darker complexions. There's this idea—borne of the clichéd image of aging expats hooking up with youthful bargirls, who, as far as many Indonesians are concerned, look like they should be working in the rice fields—that all Western men actually have a preference for women with darker skin. For many middle class Indonesian girls—who spend a fortune on skin-whitening beauty products—it's an utterly inexplicable notion. I always do my best to take the assertion in good humor, and to counter it by pointing out that it's not that your average Western guy—or girl for that matter—has a preference for darker partners; it's just that they don't care about what color you are. I don't think anyone ever believes me when I tell them this.

Speaking of forthright and inappropriate questions, they're something you have to get used to as a foreigner in Indonesia. It's not unusual, within five minutes of meeting someone for the first time, for them to have asked your age, your religion, and your monthly income—which in my country, Britain, are precisely the three questions you should never ask anyone! Ever! Maybe not even if you're in a romantic relationship with them! There's no point getting annoyed by this—they're questions Indonesians are always asking each other. I usually try laughing, and good-naturedly explaining what terrible taboos those subjects are where I come from. People usually express very sincere interest in this piece of information. Then they ask me the three questions again...

Senior Indonesian and US military officers getting on fine during an international naval exercise.

their *pribumi* counterparts (pribumi is itself a very loaded word, technically meaning "indigenous", but to all intents and purposes meaning "non-Chinese"), so it's inevitable that a certain amount of grumbling prejudice continues. But legal restrictions on Chinese language and culture are long gone; Chinese New Year is now a national holiday; and many educated Indonesians are now careful to use the term *Tionghoa* for Chinese-Indonesians, instead of the cruder *Cina*—a first step on the road to political correctness, perhaps.

A NATION OF LINGUISTS

Indonesia might be home to hundreds of different languages, but you only need to speak one of them to talk to people from the tip of Sumatra to the borders of Papua New Guinea: Bahasa Indonesia, otherwise known simply as "Indonesian". But what is this language so many foreigners insist on calling "Bahasa"? Is it easy? And do Indonesians speak English?

Bahasa Indonesia means "Indonesian Language". *Bahasa* just means "language", so when, as so often happens, someone asks "do you speak Bahasa?" the logical response is "which one?" You can call it Bahasa Indonesia or you can call it Indonesian; but you shouldn't call it "Bahasa". Good to have that cleared up!

Indonesian was originally known as "Malay", the native language of parts of Sumatra and what is now mainland Malaysia, but used as a lingua franca throughout the region for hundreds of years. During Indonesia's struggle for independence from the Netherlands it was chosen as the national language and

given its new name. Indonesian is part of the vast Austronesian language family, which spans the globe from Easter Island to Madagascar. It is gloriously acquisitive, having sucked up bits and pieces from Sanskrit, Arabic, Chinese, Portuguese, Dutch, and English over the centuries. Modern Indonesian and the other versions of Malay spoken in Malaysia and Brunei are still more or less mutually comprehensible.

THE BAHASA GAUL MAELSTROM

Formal Indonesian as taught in schools is a stiff and starchy affair, but it has a maniacal younger sibling by the name of *Bahasa Gaul*, which means

something like "Social" or "Friendly" language. At its more accessible end, Bahasa Gaul is just the colloquial version of Indonesian that people of all ages speak in casual situations, and it's fairly easy to get to grips with its basic features. Grammar gets simplified; words get abbreviated; first letters get dropped so that the much-used word *sudah*, "already", turns into *udah*. Final-syllable A turns into E, so *benar*, "true", becomes *bener*; and the expres-

---

Is Indonesian an Easy Language to Learn?

It's a statement you hear all the time from foreigners who can just about order a beer in Bahasa Indonesia: "Indonesian is the easiest language in the world!" And it's a statement that drives those who have spent years learning the language to distraction.

The idea that Indonesian is somehow uniquely easy is down to a few of its distinctive features. Like some other Asian languages, its verbs are not conjugated to create tenses, which leads to the misconception that it has no tenses at all. It has no genders; its pronouns are fixed; there are none of the tones that pose such a challenge to foreign students of Chinese; and it is written in the Roman alphabet using a delightfully consistent spelling system. Finally, there's the fact that Indonesians are

remarkably tolerant of fumbling foreigners, and very good at modifying their own speech for the sake of beginners. All this means that Indonesian really is an unusually *accessible* language for those wanting to learn a basic travelers' pidgin in a relatively short space of time. But it doesn't, unfortunately, mean it's "the easiest language in the world".

When I first came to live in Indonesia, I already had a decent grasp on the basics, thanks to three previous bouts of backpacking in the country. I was convinced that I was just a few months away from perfect fluency. In truth, I had just about reached the edge of the very wide plateau of basic functional competency, and it would be *years* before I could comfortably read an Indonesian newspaper or follow the plot of a *sinetron*.

Getting to the far side of that plateau requires a long hard slog. First up, unlike French, Spanish—or even Farsi or Hindi—Indonesian has absolutely no direct structural relationship with English, and precious little by way of common vocabulary. If you're a native English-speaker you have to learn everything from scratch, and much of it is at total odds with the hardwired concepts of your own mother tongue. And then you're faced with the overblown complexities of formal Indonesian on the one hand, and the devilish ultra-colloquialism of Bahasa Gaul on the other. This is why there are so very, very few foreigners, even from amongst the expats who've been in the country for decades, who can truly shoot the Bahasa Indonesia breeze like a native...

Left "Our City is Ready for Disasters": public education street art in Bahasa Indonesia.

Above "Please take your ticket".

Left When translation goes wrong: the Indonesian phrase here really means "stay away from drugs"!

sive particles *loh*, *kok*, *dong*, and *sih* get used incessantly.

But stray any further into the realm of Bahasa Gaul as spoken by hip young Indonesians, and you'll encounter a terrifying maelstrom of flying particles, extreme abbreviations, agglutinations, inversions, and odd bits of English chewed up and spat back out in radically modified form. It's a linguistic wall of white noise, fit to send any earnest foreign student of Indonesian fleeing in terror.

The most striking thing about this Bahasa Gaul is its sheer dynamism. It was always a rapidly evolving sort of street talk, but modern social media has given its transformative capacity a massive steroids hit, so it now shifts and reinvents itself at ridiculous speed. It's a brilliantly exciting manifestation of Indonesia's linguistic vibrancy, even if it is pretty much impossible to keep up with.

DO INDONESIANS SPEAK ENGLISH?

Educated, urban Indonesians sometimes get a bit offended when foreigners assume that Indonesians can't speak English. But though there is a tiny Jakarta-based elite who speak it at pretty much first-language level, the fact of the matter is, English just isn't spoken as widely or as well in Indonesia as it is in countries like Malaysia or India. That's not Indonesia's fault; it's down to colonial history.

Still, Indonesians definitely *want* to be able to speak English, and if you're a foreigner wandering in a place popular with tourists—Bogor's Botanic Gardens, Jakarta's Fatahillah Square, or the Borobudur temple—you *will* be pounced upon by gangs of students looking to practice their English skills. And they seem to be getting somewhere. English is definitely now more widely spoken than when I first came to Indonesia, and in the last couple of years I've started hearing trendy young Indonesians speaking English amongst themselves in cafés and shopping malls. Social media and the Internet has had a lot to do with this—the posts and comments on the average Indonesian Facebook page these days come in a glorious mishmash of English, regional languages, and Bahasa Gaul.

An Archipelago of Languages

Bahasa Indonesia might be spoken from one end of the country to the other, but it's just the start when it comes to Indonesia's linguistic make-up. There are something like 700 local languages, plus infinite dialects. The big regional languages are spoken by millions of people, and the biggest, Javanese, with nearly 100 million, has more native speakers than French. Others are the preserve of a vanishing handful. The little island of Alor in East Nusa Tenggara Province is home to just 150,000 people, but it has 15 distinct languages!

INDONESIA: THE SOCIAL MEDIA CAPITAL OF THE WORLD

A few years back I spent a night hanging out with a bunch of local mystics at an ancient temple in the mountainous wilds of East Java. Sitting outside a bamboo shack, only an oil lamp to stave off the velvety darkness, they talked to me of supernatural energy and invisible realms. It was the sort of thing that foreign travel writers love to think of as "the real Indonesia". By the time I got back to Surabaya the next day, three of the amulet-toting mystics had added me on Facebook...

Yogyakarta school kids getting online.

When I first traveled in Indonesia, "Internet" generally meant a bank of rickety old desktops in a *warnet*—a *warung Internet*, or "Internet café"— with appalling connection speeds. But these days the whole country sizzles with digital connectivity. There are housewives on Twitter and grannies on WhatsApp, and an army of commuters furiously updating their statuses in the midst of the Jakarta rush hour each morning.

INDONESIANS ONLINE
Go into just about any café in the country—from a rickety roadside coffee stall in rural Sumatra to a branch of J.CO (like Starbucks, only with added donuts) in a Jakarta shopping mall, and look at the customers. As each newcomer takes his or her seat there's an audible clunk. It's the sound of a weighty bit of Internet-ready mobile technology hitting the table where it has to sit, in line of sight at all times.

As in many countries with less than perfect infrastructure, lots of people in Indonesia skipped the stage of home

Internet connection and went straight to mobile. And it's always easier to keep up a lively Instagram account when you carry your main form of Internet access with you wherever you go. Something like 90 percent of Indonesians with personal Internet access—and there are about 100 million of them—use social media.

Another reason that's often cited for Indonesia's social media addiction— and this is quite serious—is the traffic. Jakarta alone is responsible for 2.5 percent of all the world's tweets, and most of them are probably composed while sitting stationary in the notorious *macet*, the gridlock that is one of the city's abiding features. But personally, I

think that Indonesia was always going to be a place that embraced social media with enthusiasm. Millions of Indonesians were using the long-forgotten Friendster network before anyone had ever heard of Facebook. It's all down to the fact that this is a country where social contact is as fundamental a need as food and water.

THE INDONESIAN BLOGOSPHERE
There are something like five million Indonesian bloggers, furiously posting on every topic under the sun. The handy thing for foreigners is that a surprising number of the best Indonesian blogs are written in English. There's the big cheese of the tech blogging scene, Budi Putra, the utterly awesome backpacking ladies of Indohoy, and a whole bunch of seriously glitzy fashion and lifestyle bloggers—amongst who the uncrowned queen is definitely Diana Rikasari, the woman behind the funky Hot Chocolate & Mint blog.

Unsurprisingly, the idea that you can make money—maybe even lots of it—from blogging, has caught people's attention in Indonesia. In 2014 a cannily considered video appeared online of a 21-year-old high school dropout and sometime duck herder from Semarang named Eka Lesmana, supposedly collecting his monthly 120 million-rupiah pay-out from Google AdSense at his local post office. There was a lot of excitement on social media, and young

Before There Was Facebook: friendster

I'd been working in Indonesia for barely a week when the invites started popping up in my email inbox: *Ari wants to add you on Friendster; Fitri wants to add you on Friendster...*

The forgotten social media platform Friendster was launched in California way back in 2002. It had many of the features that would eventually make Facebook such a phenomenon, but it didn't really catch on—apart from in Indonesia, that is. By the start of 2007 Friendster had something like 4 million users in Indonesia, which might not sound like much until you realize that in the entire world only 12 million people had Facebook accounts at that stage. But once the competition heated up, Friendster struggled to keep pace, and by the time it breathed its last in 2015 hardly anyone noticed its passing, not even in Indonesia.

Eka seemed to be established as something of a blogging-for-cash guru. The thing is though, the URLs of the dozen blogs he supposedly maintained were never revealed. In the world of blogging, as everywhere else, tales of impossible riches are always worth taking with a pinch of salt…

SOCIAL MEDIA AND POLITICS

Protest and activism have long been a phenomenon at the rowdier end of Indonesian politics, but these days there's usually more noise online than on the streets. In 2012 a viral Twitter hashtag—#SaveKPK—actually succeeded in prompting the then president, Susilo Bambang Yudhoyono, to weigh in on the side of Indonesia's beleaguered Corruption Eradication Commission (KPK) in a tussle with some very high-level officials. The presidential race of 2014, meanwhile, was one of the most social media-focused elections the world had ever seen. Facebook claimed to have identified 200 million election-related interactions during the campaign, and Twitter totted up 95 million election-related tweets. Inevitably, the dark side of social media was on full display

Left and above Community connectivity: "Kampoeng Cyber" is a traditional neighborhood in Yogyakarta with Wi-Fi for all, celebrated in colorful street art.

A Viral Tiger

Indonesia has a knack for online humor, often based on the most bizarre starting points. In early 2017 someone noticed that an army base at Cisewu in West Java had a very bad statue of a tiger for a mascot, snapped a photo of it, and posted it online. Within a few days hilarious memes featuring reworked images of the "Cisewu Tiger" were going viral, not only in Indonesia but around the world. The only people not to see the funny side were the soldiers. After several weeks of embarrassment they demolished the statue!

too, with a barrage of malicious online rumors about the winning candidate, Joko "Jokowi" Widodo.

The crazy thing about all of this is that still only about half of all adult Indonesians use the Internet. If the country makes this much noise while running at 50 percent capacity, imagine the roar once the rest of its citizens get online…

Diana Rikasari, Indonesia's Online Fashion Queen

One of the biggest names in the Indonesian blogosphere is the funky fashionista Diana Rikasari. Blessed with a canny command of English and a delightfully wacky sense of style, which she describes as "playful, colorful, and adventurous", she launched her Hot Chocolate and Mint blog way back in 2007. Since then she's become a veritable phenomenon, with endless awards, her own fashion line, a best-selling book, and more besides. Diana claims that the lucrative career she's built off the back of her blog was all an accident. "I never planned any of this," she says, "I didn't even know that blogs (or mine, in particular) could open so many doors." Mind you, her background in business and marketing probably helped.

These days she somehow manages to maintain the original blog plus wildly active Twitter, Instagram, and YouTube accounts, a business, and various brand ambassadorships.

"I'm very strict about time management. I have a to-do list for everything," she says.

As to just why Indonesia has such an addiction to social media, Diana has her own theory: "Indonesians really care about other people, sometimes even too much. I think most Indonesians use social media to stalk other people's lives!"

www.dianarikasari.blogspot.com

CHAPTER 2
SOCIETY AND DAILY LIFE

From the office to the schoolroom, and from Saturday night to Monday morning, it's time to take a look at Indonesian society and daily life. This is where we'll find out why Indonesian kids get so stressed at exam time, what it means to be an Indonesian feminist, how to hang out Indonesian-style, and why it's never normal to want to be on your own...

WORKADAY LIFE IN IDONESIA

When my class at primary school did a project on Indonesia we were given the idea that pretty much everyone in the country was either a pre-industrial rice farmer, or a *becak* (pedicab) driver! Needless to say, the world of work in Indonesia is a bit more complicated than that...

Traditionally, the Indonesian view of employment broke down quite simply. If you were from a poor, uneducated background you were set for a life of labor, probably on the land, and without much by the way of prospects. If you were rich, well you were rich already. And if you were somewhere in the middle, you aimed to join the public sector. The idea of a successful salaried career in the private sector was unusual: if you weren't set for hard labor or public service, and didn't already have a silver spoon in your mouth, then you went in for entrepreneurship, be it selling snacks at the side of the road, or creating a booming import-export empire.

But things began to change from the late 1960s as technological advances in agriculture suddenly freed up large numbers of one-time field laborers—especially women, who'd traditionally done much of the planting and harvesting. So where did they go? Into the factories, of course, where Indonesia's manufacturing economy was just getting going. And as the country industrialized, burgeoning financial and service sectors and a grow-

Office life at a Jakarta cable TV company.

ing consumer economy were part of the package too. There's been a bit of turbulence along the way, but these days Indonesia's economy and workforce are as diversified as anywhere—even if some people actually do still work as rice farmers or becak drivers!

A JOB FOR LIFE

For much of the 20th century the most attractive employment prospect was a position in the ranks of Indonesia's vast body of state employees which included military, police, and the sprawling apparatus of the *Pegawai Negeri Sipil*, PNS, the Civil Service. A civil service position might not be particularly well paid, but it was a job for life with lots of extra formal benefits, not least a pension. There were also, it has to be said, often opportunities for considerable illicit additional earnings in a system notorious for its institutionalized corruption. But perhaps even more importantly than the financial rewards, a civil service job brought prestige. Many of 21st-century Indonesia's solidly middle class families attained and consolidated that status through the civil service careers of previous generations.

Above Poking fun at the pegawai negeri—A cartoon mocking civil servants; the captions read "What my friends think I do. What the public think I do. What my boss thinks I do. What my parents think I do. What I think about. What I actually do."

Even today, amongst the ranks of the lower middle classes, especially in outlying provinces away from the big cities, the chance to don the olive-green civil service uniform remains a very alluring prospect, not least because of the security and prestige it offers.

LIFE IN THE KANTOR

It sometimes seems to me that the various primers and orientation courses aimed at Western expats heading to Indonesia for work do their very best to cast a pall of mystifying orientalist bunkum over the Indonesian office. Take them too seriously and you might come away with the idea that Indonesian employment is an impenetrable labyrinth of arcane eastern mysteries where nothing is as it seems. In reality there's nothing particularly exotic about the average Indonesian office, although, just like wider Indonesian society, it usually consists of a layer of easy-going warmth over a careful

Another endless round of meetings and presentations...

framework of hierarchy and respect. There's a lot of unspoken emphasis on harmony, and so being disrespectful or doing anything likely to mess with someone's hierarchical prestige will always cause problems.

The importance and respect given to formal hierarchy in Indonesian workplaces reflects the values of wider society. But I suspect it also has something to do with the fact that Indonesian office culture was originally forged in the civil service, which, like civil services everywhere, is very hierarchical indeed. Indeed, the very word "office" in Indonesian—*kantor*—still conjures up images of a dimly lit space, filled with untidy files and shuffling olive-green figures, even though these days it's more likely to refer to a bright room full of frantically motivated techies.

"Rubber Time"—Punctuality, Indonesian Style

You'll hear a heck of a lot about a concept called *jam karet* in Indonesia. It's a very well-worn cliché—something that longtime expats discourse on as if delivering the ultimate cultural insight, and that Indonesians themselves mention with a certain dash of self-parodying irony, like Irish people going on about their national love of "the craic". But there's definitely something in it!

Jam karet means "rubber time", and it refers to Indonesia's supposedly innate sense of flexibility when it comes to deadlines and fixed schedules. If the bus is an hour late, or your co-worker fails to turn up for that important meeting, it's allegedly all down to jam karet, and you'll never be able to do anything about it. Jam karet is intimately connected with another common Indonesian phrase: *nanti saja*, which means "just later". And if the reply to a question about when something's going to get done is "nanti saja", you know you've just become a victim of jam karet!

One thing that has always struck me about Indonesian workplaces, is the importance of food! In the office of the school where I first worked in Indonesia the office boys (and they're another feature of Indonesian offices— poorly paid but very obliging men who double as cleaners, runners, general skivvies and tea-makers) were continually coming in and out with takeout orders for the teachers and admin staff, and I'd find myself constantly assailed with offers

of oily snacks and sweet treats from every side. Even when I was working in a tiny newspaper office with no more than half-a-dozen coworkers, someone was always eating.

Traveling to Work

Climb aboard any long-haul bus or interisland ferry towards the end of the Muslim fasting month of Ramadan, and you'll meet them: Indonesia's millions of working class economic migrants, making what is often their only annual trip back to their home region. Economic pressures have long prompted people from all over the Indonesian archipelago to leave home in search of employment, and many regions have their own particular traditions of migration. The small towns of East Java provide many of the domestic staff for wealthy families

in Singapore, Malaysia, and the Middle East; people from the eastern regencies of Bali have been staffing cruise ships for decades; and the hard-grafting folks of Madura pop up selling sate or doing whatever else will pay in just about every corner of the country.

But there's one part of Indonesia that raises migration from an economic necessity to a rite of passage, and that's the Minangkabau region of Sumatra. Minangkabau culture is matrilineal: the women get the inheritance, so unmarried young men have always found themselves disenfranchised, and

have always gone out into the world to seek their fortune. The Minangkabau word *merantau*—which literally means something along the lines of "to go into non-Minangkabau territory"—has entered the Indonesian language as a term for migration. But the idea of merantau conveys more than just migrating for work; it invokes a sense of honorable wandering in search of wisdom as well as wealth. The reality might well be a construction site in Kuala Lumpur, but merantau is still very much a respected tradition.

YOU'LL NEVER WALK ALONE: THE SUPER SOCIABLE NATION

Apart from "Hello mister", the phrase I hear most frequently as I make my way around Indonesia is "Kok sendiri?" It's hard to give a direct translation of what's really implied by the question but it basically means something along the lines of "You're on your own??? What the hell are you doing on your own??? No, seriously, mister, what is wrong with you??? Don't you have any friends???" Because in this most social of countries, wanting to be alone is a downright deviant act.

Above Big-name brands and icy air-con—the irresistible lure of the mall!

Left Hanging out at shopping malls is a full-time occupation for some.

In Indonesia life itself is a social affair, and although this is what makes it one of the friendliest places on earth, it can cause difficulties for those who do relish a little quiet time. If I want to enjoy a peaceful Sunday afternoon on my own, I've learnt to lie when Indonesian friends message and ask what I'm up to, and more importantly, *sama siapa?*—who with? If I answer truthfully, well, you can guess the response: *kok sendiri???* And then they'll probably jump in the car and drive over to rescue me from this terrible fate...

Social life in Indonesia is a simple matter of grabbing any passing excuse to be social, to hang out. Foreigners coming to Indonesia for work sometimes complain that what is supposed to be a business meeting often turns into little more than a group hang-out, with absolutely no discussion of the matter in hand. That's partly down to a key element of business etiquette in Indonesia: an importance placed on developing personal relationships ahead

of the nitty-gritty. But it's also about the irresistible social inclination.

MALLRATS

When I first worked as a teacher in Indonesia I used to ask my Monday classes what they'd been up to over the weekend. But I soon gave up, because the answer was almost always the same: "Went to the mall…"

For many urban Indonesians of the aspiring or actual middle classes,

hanging out at the mall is the major weekend activity. I used to think it was an expression of mindless consumerism, until a colleague pointed out that most people don't actually buy anything at the mall. All those glitzy boutiques and brand outlets are really just a backdrop for the important business of being in the company of your buddies—and in a pleasantly air-conditioned setting.

CAFÉ CULTURE, INDO STYLE

I have a suspicion that Indonesia invented café culture, long before the people of the Mediterranean took to sipping espressos on shady terraces. After all, Java is a place quite literally synonymous with coffee, and a cup of the black stuff is a staple from one end of Indonesia to the other. And the cornerstone of Indonesian social life, *ngobrol* ("chatting") is always best when you combine it with *ngopi*—a lovely bit of Indonesian slang which simply means "to coffee".

Starbucks opened its first outlet in Jakarta in 2002, but local caffeine-heads

Clubbing Together

Indonesia's inclination towards social interaction is behind the country's great galaxy of clubs and "communities". There are communities for everything from fishing to heavy metal, and from mountaineering to vintage vehicles, in just about every city in the country. Some amount to little more than a Facebook page and a few bumper stickers, but many are major social organizations—albeit usually organized organically without much of a formal structure—with regular meet-ups and road-trips. On a Saturday night the streets of downtown Surabaya are often clogged with the city's myriad motorbike "communities", groups bonded only by ownership of a single type of bike, be that Vespa or Vario, Harley or Honda, but using that connection as an excuse to hang out together.

"The Small Change of Friendship"

The author Nigel Barley brilliantly describes cigarettes as "the small change of friendship" in Indonesia—offered endlessly between old buddies and new acquaintances. And as a non-smoker I'm always at a distinct social disadvantage, for this is a country where something like 70 percent of adult men smoke. The major domestic tobacco manufacturers—companies like Djarum, Dji Sam Soe, Gudang Garam, and the Philip Morris-owned Sampoerna—are amongst the biggest businesses in the country. They spend millions of dollars on highly sophisticated advertising campaigns, each company with multiple cigarette brands delicately targeted at different demographics, from aspirational urban creatives to good ol' boys back in the kampung. And while there are some official restrictions, tobacco money plays a huge role in the entertainment industries in Indonesia. The classic style of Indonesian cigarette is the *kretek*—clove-flavored, accounting for well over 80 percent of all domestic tobacco sales, and adding an unmistakably evocative fragrance to the atmosphere of Indonesian public spaces.

quickly realized that they could do better themselves, and in the last decade independent coffee shops with serious hipster cred have become a boom industry. The best ones in Jakarta, Surabaya, and Yogyakarta could easily give their New York rivals a run for their money.

But still, my own preferred places for ngopi and ngobrol would have to be the ones that were already a part of life in Indonesia long before anyone knew what a barista was. On the most scenic bends of mountain roads you'll find bamboo shacks where the seating arrangements are *lesehan*-style—you lounge on the floor at low tables—and where you can order a steaming cup of local coffee sweetened with a great dollop of condensed milk. It might not have the finesse of a barista-crafted flat white, but it tastes just as good.

HITTING THE TOWN ON MALAM MINGGU

It's *malam minggu*—literally "Sunday eve", i.e., Saturday night—and it's time to hit the town. A low-key malam minggu with friends typically features a bout of general *jalan-jalan*, wandering around. Ideally someone has a car.

There might be some mall time early on; there will definitely be food at some point; and things might end up with a long stretch of general ngobrol over coffee—in either a hipster café, or an old-school street-side hang-out, depending on how trendy, or how moneyed, your crew is. And that might well be it—unless, of course, you're hanging out with some proper party animals, in which case you'll need to be prepared to venture into the gloom of the Indonesian nightlife scene.

Bars and clubs in Indonesia do have a tendency to be divided between outrageously pricey and pretentious lounges where the indolently rich sip extravagantly priced cocktails, and a gritty netherworld of sticky dancefloors and vice. A happy medium does exist in most bigger cities, but if you're looking for afterhours drinking in small-town Indonesia you will be heading for some decidedly rough and ready places.

But then, of course, there's Jakarta, which has long had a reputation as one of the best places in Asia for nightlife. The central and southern part of the city, stretching southwards from the traffic and commerce hub of Plaza Indonesia, is home to an ever shifting array of seriously sophisticated clubs and bars where you might not want to order a drink unless you've got very deep pockets. Head the other direction, meanwhile, northwards towards the sea, and you'll descend into a world of mind-boggling sleaze, even though the original linchpin of the North Jakarta scene, the monumental den of iniquity known as Stadium, has now closed its dark doors.

Beer, handphone and cigarette— classic malam minggu ingredients!

"DO YOU LIVE IN A MUD HUT?"

No one in Indonesia lives in a mud hut; they'd get washed away by the monsoon. "Do you live in a bamboo hut, then?" That's an actual conversation I had more than once while living in Indonesia with folks back home in the UK, where some people genuinely struggled to come to terms with the fact that I lived in an actual house, with walls, windows, doors and everything!

Below Modern minimalism and traditional touches mix in an upscale villa in Bali.

It's true that there are a few people, out in the deep countryside, who really do live in bamboo huts. And there are also a good few people who live in ramshackle shanties. But generally speaking home for Indonesians—rural and urban, from Sabang to Merauke, and across a wide social spectrum—is a modern house, almost always single-story, with concrete walls and a tiled roof. But while the typical Indonesian home might not tally up with some people's exotic imaginings, it does have some distinctly Indonesian characteristics.

A HOME AWAY FROM HOME

The first house I lived in in Indonesia stood at the end of a quiet cul-de-sac in the vast suburban acreage of eastern Surabaya. It was the archetypal middle class dwelling, with a heavy green gate in front, a garage to the left, and a narrow porch opening to a cool space beyond. Immediately inside the front door was a long room, stretching right to the back of the house, with a sofa, TV, and dining table in the middle. Three bedrooms and a bathroom opened directly into this communal space. At the very back, tucked discreetly to the side, was the kitchen, and beyond that was a tiny yard, and opening onto that tiny yard was an even tinier bedroom where Sutinah, the maid, lived. That's right: the *maid*; we had a maid; I'll talk about that later.

I've lived in various other Indonesian houses in the years since, and they are almost always a variation on this simple theme. The emphasis is always on being in the company of others, and that's

Left An old-school middle-class home in Jakarta of the kind rapidly giving way to modern villas and apartments.
Below A typical Indonesian living room.

what that space at the heart of the house is for—hanging out with your family.

BEING AN ANAK KOS

When a young Indonesian leaves the warm cocoon of the family home to head for college or work in some far-off city, they don't end up living on their own in a studio apartment. They move into something called a *rumah kos*. This is usually translated as

"boarding house"—which conjures up grim Dickensian visions of gruesome landladies and drafty corridors. But

Oh Mandi! The Indonesian Bathroom

Traditional Indonesian *kamar mandi*, "bathrooms", aren't quite the same as what you might find back home. For a start, they don't usually have a bath. What they do have, though, is a big tiled tank called a *bak mandi*, full of unheated water, with a little plastic scoop for sloshing it over yourself—which is how you take a shower, Indonesian style. It's actually both quicker and more refreshing on hot days than standing under the

meager trickle of an underpowered showerhead (though these days, modern middle class homes usually do have a conventional shower as well). Traditional squat toilets are vanishing from middle class homes, replaced by sit-down flushing toilets, usually with a sort of squirting hose contraption in lieu of toilet paper—you'll get used to it!

Helping Hands:
The Pembantu

"You have a *maid*???" exclaim my British friends when I'm living in Indonesia. "You *don't* have a maid???" exclaim my Indonesian friends when I'm living in the UK...

Having live-in domestic staff is as much a middle class necessity in Indonesia as having a television. I've met Indonesians who simply can't comprehend that while I was growing up my parents—a teacher and a journalist—not only didn't have a maid; they couldn't possibly have afforded one. "But who did the housework?" they ask, aghast, and when I tell them they're still more incredulous: "Your *dad*???" Wages for domestic staff are very low in Indonesia (the attraction for young women from poor rural backgrounds is that with room and board provided you can, in theory, save everything you earn), so even families on relatively modest incomes can often afford at least one maid. Those with more cash to spare might have a whole gang of them.

The Indonesian word for maid is *pembantu*, which literally means "helper"—a somewhat softer concept than "servant"—and in many middle class households the pembantu is almost a member of the family.

the classic rumah kos is usually just a family home with space for a lodger or two. And the classic *ibu kos* ("landlady") is less a gimlet-eyed Victorian tyrant than a surrogate mother—though she'll certainly keep a close check on her lodgers, particularly if they happen to be girls (most respectable rumah kos only take lodgers of a single sex). There are also purpose-built rumah kos, which are more like budget hotels with a dozen or more identical rooms, but they're not such nice places to live, and they don't always have such wholesome reputations.

I've been an *anak kos* ("lodger", literally "boarding house kid")—a couple of times—and they were great places,

full of that unmistakable Indonesian social warmth. It's almost impossible to find a house for a short-term lease in Indonesia, but your board in a rumah kos is paid by the month. For economic or educational migrants from poor backgrounds a budget rumah kos is the only affordable accommodation option, but around the swanky private universities in major Indonesian cities you'll find rumah kos complete with swimming pools and monthly rent that runs into the hundreds of dollars. The main attraction of these places is the chance to live communally, to find a home away from home—because in Indonesia a house without other people in it is no home!

Floor-level seating, tea, snacks and cigarettes—the essential elements of hospitality in a traditional home.

A THIRST FOR LEARNING, BUT AN EDUCATIONAL SYSTEM THAT OFTEN FALLS SHORT

It's an image that defines the Indonesian morning. From straggling villages on far-flung islets to classy suburban compounds, the roads are alive with noisy chatter of 55 million children heading for school. They go in early—usually at 7.30am—and they're generally done by early afternoon when the flow reverses, the same neatly uniformed horde fanning out towards food stalls, hang-out spots, and homes.

Above Heads down! Struggling through the dreaded Ujian Nasional.

All Indonesians are supposed to go through 12 years of compulsory schooling. From the ages of six to 11 children attend *Sekolah Dasar*, Elementary School, usually abbreviated to SD. Kids in SD wear white and brick-red uniforms, and they definitely set the color scheme of the Indonesian streets first thing in the morning. After that it's on to *Sekolah Menengah Pertama* or SMP, Junior High School, for three years. The uniform for SMP is usually white and navy blue. And then there's three final years of *Sekolah Menengah Atas*, SMA, Senior High School, where the students wear white and slate-blue. The school year starts in mid-July, with a break in December and another break wherever the end of Ramadan (defined by the lunar calendar) happens to fall.

Remarkably, for such a vast country with a great deal of inequality, Indonesia manages very nearly 100 percent enrollment at Elementary School level. And Indonesia also manages near-universal literacy, with no meaningful disparity

between male and female literacy rates. But if that all makes it sound like an educational Eden, you might, unfortunately, have to think again.

Indonesia routinely scores appallingly in international assessments of skills amongst school children. It's a conundrum fit to make you grind your teeth: how can a country with a universal schooling system and total basic literacy do so badly? But you don't need to go very far beyond the school gates to start finding problems. For a start, Indonesian education puts an old-fashioned emphasis on rote learning and memorization of meaningless information. When I was teaching English in a private language center it often seemed that my main job was undoing all the damage done in state schools, where kids were drilled in convoluted formal grammar by teachers who could barely speak English themselves.

Secondly, on paper Indonesia might have one of the best teacher-to-pupil

ratios on the planet (in fact, several critical World Bank reports have actually claimed that Indonesia has *too many* teachers), but that doesn't always match the reality on the ground. The country's three million teachers are mostly poorly trained, poorly paid, and poorly disciplined. They're also more likely to play truant than the kids.

Not long ago I was sitting waiting for a ferry on a small island in eastern Indonesia. The Independence Day celebrations of 17 August were just a few weeks off, and group after group of schoolkids—some of them nothing more than first-graders—came marching past in perfect formation, diligently practicing their parts in the upcoming celebratory parades, and without an adult in sight. I asked one of the older children what was going on; their teachers hadn't turned up that morning, so they'd organized themselves!

TESTING TIMES

As the month of April looms, Indonesian kids start getting decidedly twitchy at the approach of the dreaded *Ujian Nasional*, the national tests sat at the end of each of the three stages of the schooling system. These exams—which are basically tests of memorization rather than applied

Senior high school girls hanging out after class in Bali.

Left and below University students in class.

learning—put a huge amount of pressure on students. Until recently you had to pass to graduate to the next level of schooling, and the shame of failure was awful. But the weird thing is that each year the national pass rates for the Ujian Nasional are so close to 100 percent that I always find myself wondering exactly how the unfortunate 0.5 percent have actually managed to fail. The problem, of course, is institutionalized cheating on a quite spectacular scale—often with the collusion of teachers who are as terrified of poor results as the kids.

There are those who are trying to improve the education system. When President Joko Widodo was elected in 2014, he handed command of the Culture and Education Ministry to experienced educationalist Anies Baswedan, who set out on a program of reform (his progressive reputation was later tainted by his victory in a dirty fight for the Jakarta governorship). But it'll be a long time before all the problems are ironed out. One of the unfortunate upshots of this is that those with cash to burn take their children out of the system altogether—sending them to privately run international schools at home or abroad, and then packing them off for university education overseas. This is creating a tiny youthful elite, speaking fluent English with an American twang and enjoying an outlook that places them poles apart from even the smartest of their stay-at-home compatriots.

STUDENT LIFE

Those who do make it through to the far side of high school go on to university. There are around 3,500 universities across the country, the vast majority of them privately run. As with so much else, gengsi comes into higher education in a very big way. Extravagantly overproduced studio portraits of sons and daughters in their graduation gowns adorn the walls of many Indonesian homes, and just how much prestige these images are worth is directly related to which university awarded the degree. The best of the hundred-odd state universities carry particular kudos (though none get much of an international ranking)—Gajah Mada in Yogyakarta (UGM), The Bandung Institute of Technology (ITB), The University of Indonesia in Jakarta (UI), and Airlangga in Surabaya (Unair). In the private sector, however, it's hard

to avoid the suspicion that the relative prestige often has more to do with the scale of the course fees than the academic standards.

Being a student in Indonesia does, however, earn you a certain level of well-deserved honor. The student community has had a role on the national stage since the early days of modern Indonesia. ITB in Bandung was a hot-house of the independence movement in the 1920s; the vast student protest movement was a decisive factor in the seismic shifts that brought an end to the New Order regime in 1998; and Indonesia's huge student community continues to give rise to movements for social change.

I lived for a while close to the main UGM campus in Yogyakarta—a city with no fewer than 21 individual universities, plus various further education institutes and colleges. It was a brilliantly bustling neighborhood with a permanent hum of lively conversation. It also had an epic array of cheap and tasty food and trendy cafés. British students might spend most of their extensive leisure time in an alcohol-induced stupor, but their Indonesian counterparts tend to stick to the much more sensible business of eating, coffee-drinking, and conversation.

Women in Indonesia: An Interview with Devi Asmarani of Magdalene.co

It's always difficult to make sweeping statements about the position of women in Indonesia. On the one hand, Indonesian women work; they study; they run businesses; they are elected to government. At a glance they don't seem like an oppressed gender. But on the other hand there are powerful undercurrents of religious and social conservatism, weak legal protection and many other challenges. I'm neither Indonesian, nor a woman, so I thought it would be useful to get some insight about these issues from someone who's both.

Devi Asmarani

Devi Asmarani is the chief editor of Magdalene.co, an online magazine which she set up with fellow journalist Hera Diani in 2013. It's one of the most interesting and taboo-busting of all Indonesia's media outlets, with articles—most in English—on many edgy subjects which you'll rarely see discussed in the mainstream press, including race, sexuality, and above all, women's issues. I asked Devi to share her thoughts.

Why did you decide to start Magdalene?

We realized there was a gap in the choice of popular reading for women who wanted to read something of substance, a publication that provides a different perspective when it comes to women-related issues. We thought we could offer a certain edge that other Indonesian media didn't have.

There's no way you could write and have a healthy and nonjudgmental conversation in the mainstream media about not wanting to have children, or about being gay and an observant Muslim, or about growing up being told your breasts were too big and you need to cover them up only to find out later that it's OK to have big boobs. There is a very strong sense of self-censorship that we don't encourage at Magdalene.

How do you see the situation with regards to women's rights in Indonesia today?

Not as good as it should be. I'm worried about the growing religious conservatism that has had negative implications for women in many parts of Indonesia. There are real concerted efforts to keep women in the domestic domain. There are 365 legislative products of local governments across Indonesia that discriminate against women or have implications on women's freedom of mobility or expression. Many of these bylaws were issued in towns and districts in Aceh, West Sumatra, West Java, and Sulawesi.

I also think that not enough resources are being channeled to address the basic issues when it comes to women's rights. There is the insistence to maintain the legal marrying age at 16 (when even the Indonesian law on child protection defines a child as someone below the age of 18). And there is still poor handling of sexual violence, while a weak legal system lets the perpetrators off easily. Female single parents also often still face challenges in obtaining legal or social protection.

I'm usually pretty positive when describing the position of women in Indonesia to other foreigners; do you think I should be more critical?

Yes, you should be. Do Indonesian women have a high level of empowerment and equality? Yes, when compared to some other countries in Asia and the Middle East. But there is a lot of room for improvement.

So what are the biggest things that still need to change when it women's rights in Indonesia?

For one, the whole government structure must have strong training on gender perspective to mainstream gender equality across all levels of the bureaucracy, law enforcement, and the legislative bodies. Right now, women's issues, including women's rights and protection, are seen as the scope of only one ministry: the Ministry of Women's Empowerment and Child Protection.

This is very important in the efforts to reduce violence against women, but

its implication will be seen in all areas from education to workplace, from the public domain (including the media) to the domestic domain. It will definitely empower women and allow for more conversation on gender inequality.

Some Westerners seem to think "Islam" and "women's rights" are incompatible, and worry about the fact that more Indonesian women are adopting Muslim dress codes. But I get the impression that in Indonesia it's sometimes possible for Muslim women to become more religiously observant, and more empowered at the same time. Do you have any thoughts on this?

You're quite right on this one. What I love about Indonesian feminists who come from religious backgrounds is that they see their religious credentials as empowering assets to help them bring about change from within. They are informed and they are critical and, in a way, they are so much better at fighting patriarchy (and definitely so much more courageous) in a religiously conservative society than the rest of us, who can only criticize from "the outside".

But one must also be cautious when applying this to the general trend of hijab-wearing women in Indonesia. I see the growing tendency of women wearing hijab as an issue of conformity. We are quite a communal people who generally loathe to be different. I find that some women feel pressured to wear the hijab because everyone in their family, or everyone in their workplace, or in their neighborhood, or in their social circle wear it.

I also find it a bit shocking that some people my age, middle class women, have even grown more conservative than our parents' generations. They start making their children wear the hijab earlier, which is very problematic, because as the girls grow up and start to question their identity or want to express themselves authentically by removing their veil, people, even those who don't wear the hijab, see it as an act of betrayal. They have to be extraordinarily brave to remove the hijab.

What does it mean to be an Indonesian feminist? Does Indonesian feminism have its own unique characteristics?

This is a tough question that I have pondered for some time. I have met so many Indonesian feminists who would

not fit the tired and clichéd stereotypes of angry feminists. I find that Indonesian feminists are very good at living and working in that gray area that separates patriarchy and feminism. They are empowered but they are very good at navigating within the social and religious confines without unnecessary hostilities. It's like they choose their battles carefully.

Final question: Kartini—the aristocratic Javanese woman who pioneered education for girls and wrote on women's issues at the turn of the 20th century—is a national hero and still the best-known symbol of the women's movement. On 21 April each year, schoolgirls across the country get done up in traditional Javanese dress to honor her memory. Is she really still a useful icon for women's rights in modern Indonesia?

I will have to say, yes. However, she would be a more useful icon if her actual significance hadn't been so diluted throughout history, and by the ridiculous *kebaya*-wearing celebration we do every year. Kids grow up never really knowing her significance, never once reading any of her writings.

Her significance to me is not that she opened up the girls' school (though that was important, too), but the fact that she showed that even in those years, a Javanese woman could have such sophisticated critical thoughts and ideas, and could articulate them. I think Indonesian women, specifically middle class young women, need this kind of hero to inspire them, although the millennials might find it hard to relate to this quiet strength.

DATING, SEX AND MARRIAGE

The Internet is awash with articles claiming to offer definitive insights into the world of dating in Indonesia. But they are usually written by expat men, and they seem to focus almost exclusively on the kind of dating that originates in the seedy bars of Jakarta's notorious Blok M quarter. There are also plenty of more formal, anthropologically-inclined articles which paint a portrait of a deeply traditional society where all aspects of courtship are overseen by conservative parents, where holding hands in public is forbidden, and where premarital sex is completely unknown (beyond the boundaries of Blok M, presumably). It shouldn't take a genius to work out that these contradictory portrayals in truth represent opposing extremes, and don't really have much to do with how most young Indonesians go looking for love.

Above Weddings are an excuse for extravagant traditional dress, as with this Balinese couple.

It didn't take me long when I started teaching English to Indonesian teenagers to realize that they were pretty much like teenagers everywhere. There was always plenty of gossip about romances blossoming between classmates; someone was always broken-hearted; and the girls were forever huddled in a corner dissecting the latent romantic inferences extractable from a text message.

The first step on the road to forming a romantic attachment is *pendekatan*. This is a gentle process of "getting close" to your potential beau in general social settings. Mind you, Indonesians tend to move fast: a couple of trips to the mall as part of a group of friends and a subsequent flurry of text messaging is all that's needed before formal *pacar* (the gender-neutral word for boyfriend/girlfriend) status is achieved. And from then on, it's time for *pacaran* (dating, with a specific person; dating in general is *perkencanan*), which typically involves going to the movies, hanging out in coffee shops and at food stalls, and, inevitably, going to the mall.

For young people, still living with their parents—and especially for girls—life is definitely a bit more restrictive in Indonesia than it is in most Western countries—probably comparable to how things were in the USA a couple of generations ago. It would certainly be very, very unusual for an unmarried young couple to be allowed to share a bed under their parents' roof. But at the same time, there's an awful lot of parental blind-eye-turning going on, and it certainly seems to have become more socially acceptable for university-age couples to take backpacking trips together. All of which, brings us conveniently to the topic of sex…

SEX AND SEXUALITY

According to public morality—and according to those anthropological primers—premarital sex just isn't allowed and doesn't happen in Indonesia. But of course, wherever you are in the world, public morality has never really tallied with what people actually do. There are great variations between different communities, different regions, and different religious outlooks, but there's certainly nothing particularly unusual about premarital sex in Indonesia. More than quarter of a century ago, one study revealed that over 50 percent of unmarried couples in urban areas were having sex, and it would be a safe bet to say that the percentage has increased considerably since then. Unmarried cohabitation is still highly unusual, however, and having children outside of marriage likewise. Unmarried (as opposed to divorced) mothers face a good deal of stigma in most parts of Indonesia. It's unfortunate that sex education is rather lacking. I've been to a depress-

The happy couple dressed in the traditional Minangkabau wedding costume from West Sumatra.

Below Regional ethnic identity comes to the fore on the wedding day for a Batak couple in Sumatra.

Above The happy modern family.

Below Indonesia loves a celebrity wedding—like this one, between sinetron star Selena Alesandra and the young politician Febry Nara.
Bottom The big day.

ing number of wedding ceremonies for what in Indonesia are known as "marriages by accident"—where the bride is displaying a distinct bump beneath her wedding dress...

TYING THE KNOT

If the dating scene in Indonesia is more liberal than many foreigners might imagine, marriage is still a very important thing, and choosing to remain unmarried is, for both men and women, something akin to a deviant act—and certainly something that will result in incessant hectoring from parents, aunts and uncles, and society at large. The question in Indonesia is not "Are you married?", but "Are you married *yet*?" And if the answer is "Not yet," then the next question is, inevitably, "Why not?"

A young couple don't have to be going steady for very long before the wedding question comes up, and older generations still look on an unmarried woman of 25 as very nearly an old spinster. And liberal parental attitudes towards dating will often take a markedly more conservative turn as soon as marriage is on the cards. Even the most apparently secular families will often balk at the prospect of their offspring marrying someone of another religion, and they might also be thoroughly disapproving of someone judged to be socially inferior—and formal parental approval is generally an essential part of the process.

Wedding customs vary wildly across religions and ethnicities in Indonesia, but these days you'll often encounter a sort of hybrid of Western style and local traditions, complete with flamboyant white wedding dresses and multi-tiered wedding cakes. There's also the Indonesian marriage essential known by the English term "prewed". Not content with the already extravagant professional photography on the day itself, no modern Indonesian couple (or their parents) could be happy without an additional set of similarly extravagant pre-wedding photos of the couple. At the very least these will be formal studio portraits, but for the wealthiest people there are "pre-wed packages" that might include an all-inclusive trip to a resort in Bali and a feature-length video of the bride-and groom-to-be cavorting in romantic clifftop locations.

MIXING IT UP

Everyone in Indonesia has to have an official religious affiliation, listed on their identity card, regardless of whether they actually bother practicing the faith in question. And since 1974 every married couple is technically supposed to be of the same religion, meaning that if, for example, a Muslim wants to marry a Catholic, one or other of them has to convert. You'll often hear it claimed that the conversions in cases like this are almost always to Islam, as both the majority Indonesian religion, and, allegedly, a more chauvinistic tradition. But my own observations of various families I know in Java suggest that this is nonsense. What decides the direction of conversion is more likely to be the relative religiosity of the two families involved (there are plenty of avowedly non-practicing Indonesian Muslims, as well as plenty of devoutly church- or temple-going Christians, Buddhists, and Hindus), and, perhaps more importantly, their relative social status. In short, the richest, most prestigious set of in-laws are more likely to see the conversion going in their direction.

It's also possible for a mixed couple to get around the rules altogether if there's no real pressure from their families. With the help of an obliging religious official, a marriage can be carried out on a promise of future conversion, but once the rings have been exchanged and the certificates signed there's no one keeping check. I know one couple in East Java where the woman, a non-practicing Muslim, agreed to convert to her husband's Catholic faith, and a promise was made that he would guide her into her new religion after their wedding. However, he's never been much of a church-goer himself, and he also declares himself singularly *malas*—"lazy"! Twenty years later she's still, technically, a Muslim.

Being Gay in Indonesia

The position of LGBT people in Indonesia is full of unsettling contradictions. On the one hand this is a country where homosexuality has never been illegal. It's a place where, historically, transgender people have frequently been more visible than in Europe—albeit often only as sex workers. And it's also a place where campy flamboyance and saucy double entendres have always gone down well with television audiences. Then, on the other hand, it's a country with a censorious public morality and undercurrents of severe religious conservatism, and where homosexuality is considered sinful by many, even those who would happily laugh along with a comedic cross-dresser on TV.

There are sporadic outbursts of outright public hostility to the LGBT community. In a weird and disturbing bout of moral panic which seemed to come surging out of nowhere in early 2016, several senior politicians made homophobic public statements—including calls for gay people to be banned from university campuses—and a storm of anti-LGBT rhetoric was cooked up on mainstream social media. At the height of the outburst the national broadcasting commission actually issued a directive telling Indonesian TV stations not to feature men with "effeminate hand gestures and speaking styles" in their schedules—a move seemingly designed to bring many a successful broadcasting career to an end.

Despite hostility of this sort, however, there is still a very lively gay social scene in Indonesia's bigger cities; social media offers endless opportunities for social and romantic connections; and amongst the educated, liberally-minded middle classes there's a reasonable degree of acceptance. For many gay Indonesians the hardest part of life is not any threat from oppressive officialdom or religious zealots, but the difficulty in finding true acceptance from parents. A good number of gay people in Indonesia who are open about their sexuality with friends and colleagues still feel completely unable to come out to their parents, and in this family-obsessed country there is always pressure to conform and find a spouse of the opposite sex. For some brilliant first-hand insight into these issues check out articles by the writer who goes by the name of "Downtown Boy" on the Magdalene.co website; his pieces are often hilariously funny, but also utterly heartbreaking.

THE DARK SIDE: INDONESIA'S UNDERBELLY

It's safe to say that many Indonesians—of all socio-economic backgrounds—have a grossly inflated sense of the level of crime and disorder in their own country. Time and again while on my solo motorbike road trips, locals met along the way express concern for my wellbeing. Am I not afraid of the "bad people" who allegedly haunt the roads of the republic, they want to know (and also, seriously mister, kok sendiri???). And when I tell people that in all honesty I feel much more threatened walking through virtually any city in Britain late at night than I have ever felt in Indonesia, they tend to express outright disbelief.

Where exactly this exaggerated fear comes from, in what most objective outsiders agree is a very safe country, is hard to explain. I've heard it claimed that it's a legacy of the years of undemocratic rule under Suharto's New Order regime, when the authorities supposedly encouraged a climate of fear. The idea was that people would give the authoritarian rulers their backing as the only defense against the mythical hordes of "bad people". I'm not entirely sure if this is true, but I do know that Indonesians aren't always the best people to ask for advice about travel safety in their own country, unless you want to end up a paranoid wreck!

CRIME AND VIOLENCE

There is crime, of course—plenty of it. But it's almost all of a petty sort, and it's rarely violent. I used to work gathering news stories from the local Indonesian-language press for a weekly English-language newspaper in Bali, and my daily reading consisted of an endless litany of small thefts, pickpocketing, bag-snatchings, and occasionally inept convenience store robberies. The most worryingly dangerous manifestation of this petty criminality comes in the form of motorbike bag snatching. This is actually the only crime I've ever had firsthand experience of in Indonesia. One night in Surabaya I was giving a friend a lift home on my motorbike, and as we approached an intersection a pair of skinny youths clipped past us

Top Bad memories of street violence in Jakarta in the 1990s when a collapsing economy and discontent with an autocratic regime led to unrest, especially in the capital city.

Below Voices in the wilderness—a demonstrator demands an end to corruption.

Above and middle Behind bars in Jakarta. Indonesia has a national prison population of well over 200,000, with numbers rising sharply in recent years thanks to crackdowns on illegal drugs.

and tried to grab my companion's bag. They didn't manage to get it, and they didn't pull us off the bike, but it left me shaken. Mind you, in fifteen years of wandering right, left, and center all over the country that's my one and only experience of "bad people in the road"—which is pretty good going.

METH MADNESS

Years ago, an Indonesian friend ashamedly confessed to me that her parents were struggling to deal with her twenty-something brother's drug-taking. She was from a nice, middle class family, so when I asked, "What kind of drugs," I was picturing the guy puffing on a bit of cannabis in his bedroom. "I'm not sure," she replied; "the one that looks like little crystals…"

Crystal-methamphetamine is a big thing in Indonesia. The underground nightlife scene of North Jakarta might be awash with ecstasy; cocaine might be on the table at certain high-class parties in Bali; and ganja grown in Aceh in the far north of Sumatra might pop up everywhere. But the substance that defines Indonesia's drug scene is the singularly nasty concoction that is crystal-meth, known locally as *shabu-shabu*. Exactly how many people use it

Hello Dolly

For years, when I told Indonesians in other parts of the country that I lived in Surabaya, all too often they'd respond with a knowing leer: "Dolly, mister; I bet you go to Dolly every night..." Dolly was the East Java capital's notorious red light district, supposedly named after a colonial-era madam. It was Indonesia's best known example of *lokalisasi*, semi-official tolerance zones where the authorities could keep an eye on organized prostitution (and extort money from the brothel keepers, it was widely rumored), and

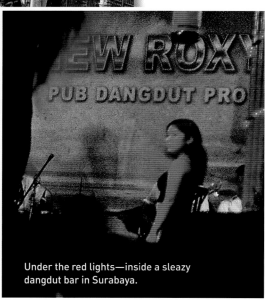

Under the red lights—inside a sleazy dangdut bar in Surabaya.

Above The boys in brown—Brimob, the Indonesian police's elite Mobile Brigade, ready for action.

is unknown (though the official estimate of all habitual drug users nationwide is 4.2 million), but it seems to span the whole of society. Celebrities have been caught with it. Airline pilots have been caught with it. Even judges and policemen have been caught with it. And while Indonesia has a notoriously hardline legal stance on drugs, with the death penalty on the statute books for smuggling and very long jail terms for possession, a lack of rehabilitation facilities and education means the issue just won't go away.

RED LIGHT NIGHTS

Prostitution is a strange sort of open secret in Indonesia—ostensibly at absolute odds with the public morality of a country where religious and family values are sacrosanct, but at the same time quite spectacularly widespread, not very well hidden, and discussed openly and unashamedly in all-male company in a way that would never be normal where I come from. The seedy bars of Jakarta's Blok M, and Surabaya's now defunct Dolly red light district have nationwide notoriety, but there's not a town in the country that doesn't have a clutch of shabby cafés somewhere on the outskirts, where there's more on offer than warm Bintang beer

and a tinny dangdut soundtrack—and where, disturbingly, HIV infection rates are steadily climbing.

KKN: THE REAL DARK SIDE

While drugs, crime, and prostitution might be topics to set the conversation ablaze at roadside coffee stalls, most Indonesians will ultimately agree that the country's real dark side comes in the form of KKN. Indonesians love an acronym, and this one stands for *korupsi, kolusi, nepotisme*, which doesn't really need much translation, but for the record it's "corruption, collusion, nepotism".

where, more positively, NGOs could look out for the women and make concerted efforts to combat the spread of HIV.

I went there, once—at the behest of a magazine editor who wanted an article about what claimed to be "the biggest red light district in Southeast Asia", I should add! I took my Canadian housemate along for moral support, and we found not the glittering pleasure-palace of popular imagination, but a couple of scrappy streets where bored-looking women lounged behind the windows of shabby "guesthouses". We had a beer in a dingy *dangdut* bar, and went home.

Dolly, however, has had its day. In 2015 Surabaya's otherwise generally progressive mayor ordered the whole quarter shut down in the name of public morality. The 1,500 resident sex workers were dispersed, and the thousands of people who made a living in the attendant service industries were left jobless. Appalled campaigners and NGO workers claim that prostitution has now been dispersed across the shadier corners of the city, where the women are beyond the reach of their help.

Indonesians love to moan about the corruption that's endemic in their homeland. Indeed, they often descend to hyperbole and a weird sort of self-reflexive racism when they warm to the topic. They claim that Indonesia is the most corrupt country on earth (in truth it's not even close; it usually comes about halfway down the list in global corruption indexes, in the same general vicinity as India and China, and a heck of a long way above places like Somalia and Afghanistan), and that Indonesian people have some kind of special genetic predisposition to graft (outright nonsense: the Dutch colonialists who once ruled Indonesia often displayed levels of corruption that would make even the dodgiest modern Indonesian judge raise his eyebrows).

It's certainly true, though, that when it comes to politicians and the judiciary, standards are pretty woeful. The culture of kickbacks that was such a feature of the later years of the Suharto regime hasn't really gone away, and justice for those with fat wallets usually looks very different from justice for those with nothing to their name. Indonesians hate this stuff; the beleaguered efforts of the Corruption Eradication Commission, the KPK, get enthusiastic support, and demonstrators regularly call for corruptors to be executed.

But it sometimes seems to me that the same people who routinely condemn this top-level corruption, are a little blind to matters closer to home. The concept of "patronage"—of the "big guy" sharing his power and fortune with his family and community, and creating powerful bonds of mutual obligation in the process—is an old and enduring one in Indonesia. And that "big guy" can be a local mayor who repays certain favors once he's in power, or simply the senior aunty or uncle in any extended family who helps out with college fees for nieces, motorbike credit repayments for nephews, and the monthly rent for impecunious younger brothers—and who, strangely enough, often turns out to have a job in the police or the civil service…

Life inside a Jakarta prison is no picnic.

PREMAN: Indonesias Street Gangsters

The criminal underbelly of Indonesia is the domain of a certain type of man. As portrayed in popular culture, they are long-haired, tattooed, thuggish and charismatic at the same time, and quite possibly in possession of formidable prowess in martial arts and even black magic. They are *preman*, a word which comes from the Dutch *vrijman*, meaning, quite simply, "free man".

On the one hand, preman are simply petty street thugs and gangsters, but their status in popular imagination is complicated by the fact that the role of the preman occasionally blurs with that of the *pemuda*, the youthful revolutionaries who drove Indonesia's independence struggle, and of the *jago*, an older romantic figure of rural rebellion. The reality is anything but romantic, however. Keep your eyes open around any bus station or market, and you'll probably spot some low-level preman. Lounging around and looking more like gone-to-seed rock stars than svelte *pencak silat* masters, their activities generally amount to running petty protection rackets. More sinisterly, preman en masse can sometimes act as a mob-for-hire, deployed in the name of intimidation by powerful puppet masters in times of political unrest.

CHAPTER 3

INDONESIA'S VIBRANT MUSIC SCENE

Indonesia has one of the most vibrant pop music cultures on the planet. Whether we're talking manufactured talent show fodder or ferocious underground innovation, this is a nation with serious rhythm. So let's crank up the volume, delve into the Indonesian music scene, and meet with its dangdut divas, its smoke-wreathed jazzmen, its punks, and its *pengamen*.

THE MUSICAL ARCHIPELAGO

Can you hear it? For many foreign journalists and travel writers the scent of clove cigarettes is the ultimate Indonesian motif, an easy cliché with which to conjure up the atmosphere of the country. But for me it's not nicotine-laden smoke that sets the Indonesian tone; it's music. Drifting out across the archipelago from tinny stereos in rattletrap buses; from state-of-the-art sound systems in hipster coffee shops; from crackling PAs in greasy underground rock clubs; live and unamplified from a thousand street-corner hangouts; and from the speakers of a million mobile phones: this is the most musical nation on earth. If all you know of Indonesian music is gamelan, prepared to have your horizons widened!

International hipsters have a thing for vinyl, but in Jakarta the must-have retro music format is the cassette.

FROM PUNK ROCKERS TO POP PRINCESSES

Indonesia's musical diversity is staggering—and I'm not talking about gamelan orchestras and mysterious folk traditions; I'm talking about modern popular music. From avant garde jazz to heavy metal, you'll find just about every genre imaginable on offer here—and done as well as or better than back home. Imported music does get some attention—and big-name international touring acts do stop by in Jakarta. But Indonesia has a musical confidence which means that its punk bands and its pop princesses, its folkies and its bluesmen all sound entirely authentic and original.

Unsurprisingly, Indonesian music is a major export to neighboring countries with cultural connections, and many Indonesian stars are household names in Singapore and Malaysia too. In fact, a few years back the Malaysian music industry employees' union actually called for a legal limit on the Indonesian releases that dominate their country's charts. Beyond Southeast Asia, however, few people have ever heard of Indonesia's mega-selling musical superstars—not because their work isn't good, but because, apart from some of the underground punk bands, they almost always sing in Indonesian.

From Gamelan to Gambu: Indonesia's Traditional Music in a Nutshell

Indonesia's most famous musical form is undoubtedly the *gamelan*—the Javanese metallophone orchestra. A full gamelan ensemble might include flutes, stringed instruments, drums, and singers, but at the heart of its distinctive sound are the tuned gongs and xylophone-style instruments. Gamelan has important cultural roles—providing the backing for wayang kulit shadow puppetry and traditional dances. There are various other traditional percussion forms in Indonesia—particularly the *angklung*, a West Java specialty made of tuned bamboo tubes on a frame.

The guitars wielded by modern Indonesian rockers have their own ancient antecedents too. It was almost certainly traders from Yemen who first brought stringed, lute-style instruments to Indonesia. Known as *gambus*, you can still find these instruments today, used to play Arabic-influenced folk music. In eastern Indonesia these Middle Eastern lutes were given a local twist in the form of the *sasando*, one of the coolest, and strangest, traditional instruments I've ever seen—a 28-stringed harp made from the leaves and wood of the lontar palm.

The ultimate antecedent for the country's wealth of modern popular

Top Indonesian Tracks

A rundown of personal pop and rock favorites from my Indonesian playlist.

Hightime Rebellion, *Sail* Sophisticated indie rock from hipster Jakarta.

Ligro, *Stravinsky* Seriously out-there stuff from Indonesia's most progressive jazz-rock pioneers.

The Changcuters, *I Love You Bibeh* A grin-inducing Rolling Stones homage from everyone's favorite Bandung pranksters.

Iwan Fals, *Bongkar* A wiry classic with the veteran singer-songwriter at his most rousing.

Ungu, *Aku Datang Untuk Mencintaimu* Archetypal Indonesian soft rock chart fodder from sensitive boys with big voices.

Ratu, *Lelaki Buaya Darat* This prime piece of bubblegum pop was a big hit the first year I lived in Indonesia and it always brings back happy memories.

Steven & Coconut Treez, *Welcome To My Paradise* Indonesia has always had a bit of a thing for reggae, and Steven N. Kaligis is the local answer to Bob Marley. This UB40-esque track is a very rare example of an Indonesian English-language hit.

---

music is a style called *kroncong*. When the first Portuguese sailors turned up in Indonesia in search of spices in the 16th century, they brought their musical instruments with them—especially the small, four-stringed guitar known as the *cavaquinho* (itself a distant descendant of the Arab lute, just like the *gambus*). Like the people of Hawaii, who turned Portuguese guitars into ukuleles, the Indonesians took the *cavaquinho* to their heart. By the 19th century touring kroncong ensembles were a common Indonesian phenomenon. They typically featured a couple of ukulele-style guitars, plus violin, bass, and sometimes other strings, played in a European-style major key, but with complex interlocking rhythms showing a hint of gamelan influence. The name kroncong is an onomatopoeia, echoing the strumming of a kroncong guitar. Today kroncong music has nostalgic associations in Indonesia, played by the house bands in kitschy *tempo doeloe* ("days gone by") restaurants. But it represents a long tradition of adopting and adapting Western instrumentation, a tradition which, arguably, gives modern Indonesian popular music a maturity and confidence which is missing in the pop scenes of some other Asian countries.

Left to right Balinese temple ensemble, Jakarta Kroncong, a Sundanese singer and a gamelan player.

The **Peterporn** Scandal!

Indonesia's ultimate soft-rock heartthrob has long been Nazril "Ariel" Irham, lead singer of the band formerly known as Peterpan. He was also at the center of Indonesia's ultimate celebrity scandal when, in 2010, a couple of homemade sex tapes, apparently featuring Ariel with his then and former celebrity girlfriends, turned up on the Internet. They had reportedly been lifted from a stolen laptop, but it was Ariel himself who ended up arrested under the terms of Indonesia's controversial—and rarely enforced—anti-pornography laws. The case, inevitably dubbed "the Peterporn Scandal", was tried in Bandung, and the court was at times picketed by both mobs of angry Islamists demanding Ariel be condemned, and by gangs of hysterical teenage girls begging for their idol to be freed. He actually went to jail, and served two years.

The Indonesian gossip mill went into overdrive, and there were all sorts of rumors that the whole affair—from the stolen laptop to the courtroom—had actually been a devious revenge plot by some shadowy but all-powerful jilted husband (Ariel was alleged to have been a ladies' man of the first rank, with a string of high-class conquests a mile long). Whatever the truth, his bandmates stood by him. Once he was freed in 2012 they rebranded as Noah (supposedly under the terms of a longstanding agreement over ownership of the Peterpan name with a couple of former band members, but possibly also as a very convenient way to escape the "Peterporn" label). They're still topping the charts, and the teenage girls are still swooning over the sometime convict.

DANGDUT! INDONESIA'S UNIQUE BRAND OF WORKING CLASS POP

A rambunctious riot of diverse influences, big beats, and broken hearts, dangdut music is the soundtrack of working class Indonesia. If you spend any time stuck on public transport you may come to hate it with a passion, but there's no denying that this genre, the "music of the people", has soul.

Scantily-clad dangdut singers doing their thing.

For years I struggled to explain dangdut to the uninitiated. I could tell people that it was a distinct brand of Indonesian popular music made up of classical Malay roots, Bollywood film influences, Arabic pop, rock and roll, and goodness knows what else besides, all tossed into a sonic blender and served up at a relentlessly cantering pace. I could point out that the name dangdut was itself an onomatopoeia, echoing the sound of the *kendhang*, the tabla-style drum that's an essential part of a dangdut ensemble. And I could confess that I'd endured many an overnight bus trip, praying for salvation as an endless round of dangdut classics roared from the tinny stereo system. But none of that really conveyed what dangdut was as a cultural phenomenon.

But then it dawned on me. Dangdut is to Indonesia what country music is to the United States: a distinctive genre running parallel to mainstream pop, and a part of the very identity of the nation. What's more, just like country music, dangdut is an earthy tradition with working class associations and a lyrical focus on heartbreak. The self-proclaimed sophisticates of the middle classes tend to sneer at it. And just like country music it has plenty of feuds, scandals, and veteran stars inclined to dabble in reactionary politics...

THE ROOTS OF DANGDUT

How exactly dangdut came into being is a point of debate. Rhoma Irama, the enduring "King of Dangdut", sometime heartthrob, wannabe politician, and part-time religious zealot, has claimed that it grew fully formed out of the folk music traditions of northern Sumatra, via the *Orkes Melayu*—the

Rhoma Irama: **The King of Dangdut**

He's in his seventies now and his hair looks less convincing with every passing year; he's tangled with political scandal, earned plenty of liberal opprobrium, and been caught in a compromising situation with an actress 40 years his junior. But Rhoma Irama still clings to his crown as *Raja Dangdut*—"King of Dangdut". During the 1970s he and his sometime collaborator Elvy Sukaesih turned the genre into a popular behemoth, and he still draws the crowds. Rhoma has long been a contradictory figure, however, combining his early glam-rock style with a distinct streak of religious conservatism. By the turn of the 21st century, with a whole new generation of decidedly raunchy dangdut stars coming to the fore, he was regularly condemning the "vulgar" and "un-Islamic" behavior of the likes of Inul Daratista. His political activity had also led to controversy, with speeches that flirt with religious and racial chauvinism. He has also spoken—to the considerable alarm of some—of his own presidential aspirations.

Dangdut divas singing their hearts out with tales of passion and heartbreak.

Whatever its origins, since it first emerged in the 1970s, dangdut's rumbling rhythm has proved unstoppable. It has spawned myriad variations—not least remix treatments in the form of techno-dangdut. But the classic dangdut line-up still features a standard pop-rock ensemble with guitar, bass, and drums, plus synthesizer, flute, and the *kendhang* for the distinctive beat.

MUSIC OF THE PEOPLE

I once asked one of my language school classes in Indonesia who exactly dangdut music was for. They all sniggered. "My maid", they said, "becak drivers". This musical class snobbery has always made me look favorably on dangdut as a cultural phenomenon, even if I struggle to appreciate the music itself! Its working class associations have long made it a genre associated with a sense of no-nonsense "Indonesian pride". It's what people from the kampungs want played at their weddings, and unsurprisingly, it's what canny politicians use as a soundtrack for their campaigns. In fact, if you ever encounter a political rally in Indonesia, stick around until the speeches are over, because chances are they'll be followed by a dangdut performance, complete with "sexy dancers".

"Malay Orchestra"—genre of the mid-20th century. But you only need to hear the briefest burst of dangdut to detect the myriad other influences that are involved—not least Hindi pop. In fact, the first recorded instance of the word "dangdut" appears in the lyrics of Rhoma Irama's 1973 hit, *Terajana*, itself a homage to Indian film music.

Inul and the *Ngebor* Scandal

By the late 1990s dangdut had developed a distinct reputation for raunchiness. The most provocative moves of all belonged to one Inul Daratista, from the dusty East Java town of Pasuruan. Inul found nationwide fame in 2003—not so much for her rock-tinged dangdut songs as for her trademark onstage moves. Her distinctive dance style was christened *ngebor*, literally "drilling", and it seemed to take inspiration in equal parts from Egyptian belly dancers, Elvis Presley, and industrial machinery. Rhoma Irama and other religious conservatives were appalled. They claimed that Inul was corrupting Indonesia's youth, and cited her in their campaigns against pornography. But the controversy only helped her career, and she has since drilled her way into the ranks of dangdut royalty.

Remembering The Queen of Raunch

In 2017 Indonesia lost the most flagrantly provocative of all its dangdut stars. Julia Perez, or Jupe as she was usually known, was born Yuli Rahmawati in 1980. She had a mixed career as glamor model, singer, actress, and "condom ambassador"—though all of these roles tended to involve her taking off as many clothes as possible and saying outrageous things. In 2012 she performed a pole dance at a Jakarta intersection in celebration of having gained a million followers on Twitter, and in 2013 she spent three months in jail for assaulting fellow dangdut star Dewi Persik on the set of a horror movie. Her lyrics, meanwhile, were deliberately designed to raise pulses. The song *Jupe paling suka* ("What Jupe likes most") is a raunchy paean to the joys of "passionate 69 love", and *Belah duren* is an extended euphemism about the pleasures of "splitting a durian". However, her willingness to go head to head with enraged religious conservatives and to speak up for unfettered self-expression made her more than a tawdry professional controversialist, and when she died—of cancer, far too young, in June 2017—there was a sense, even amongst the kind of liberal sophisticates who usually sneer at dangdut, that a very bright light had gone out.

INDONESIAN ROCK AND POP ROYALTY

From shiny pop princess to men with furrowed brows, big voices, and broken hearts, and from high-octane pop-punk groups to folk-rock balladeers, Indonesia's popular music scene is a thing of glorious diversity. In fact, rather than seeming like a cut-price knock-off of Western pop, it comes across as its equal, and whether it's the manufactured chart fodder or the indie interlopers, I often find myself thinking, "If only these guys sung in English, then they could conquer the globe…"

AGNES MONICA

Indonesian pop probably has its ultimate origins in kroncong and the traveling "orchestras" of the colonial era, but the true pioneers of Indonesian pop as it is today started rocking out in the 1960s. In fact, conventional wisdom credits pretty much the whole thing to a gang of silky-voiced brothers from the small town of Tuban in East Java.

Koes Plus are often called "the Indonesian Beatles", though given that they're a family affair "the Indonesian Bee Gees" might be more appropriate. Formed way back in 1960, they were originally called Koes Bersaudara ("Koes Brothers"), until the drummer Nomo Koeswoyo was replaced by a non-family

member. Their early repertoire was largely covers of British and American rock and roll, and during one of President Sukarno's regular bouts of anti-Western posturing they were actually arrested for playing Beatles covers. By the early 1970s, however, they had hit on their own enduring formula of big hair, bigger trousers, and plodding self-penned ballads—a formula used by pretty much all of

the best-known Indonesian bands of the 60s and 70s such as Panbers and The Mercy's (misplaced apostrophes are also something of a tradition in Indonesian musical nomenclature).

One early Indonesian pop group, however, were far more radical than any bunch of flares-wearing, Beatles-covering brothers. Dara Puspita, straight out of Surabaya, were Indonesia's original all-girl rockers. Formed in 1964, they played garage rock, dressed to kill, and

freaked out the authorities with their wild onstage antics. And their music is awesome! Stripped down, rough around the edges, and driven at breakneck pace by fearsome drummer Suzy, tracks like *A Go Go* and *Pip Pip Yeah!* sound almost like a prototype, female version of the Ramones. Dara Puspita actually toured Europe for several years in the late 60s, but they broke up in 1972. As far as I'm concerned they were Indonesia's first indie heroes.

MODERN POP AND ROCK

By the turn of the 21st century, as Indonesia emerged from the post-Suharto *Reformasi* period into democracy, its music industry was a massive, multifaceted monster, with every imaginable genre represented. There are, though, certain styles that seem eternally overrepresented in the Indonesian musical mainstream. Naturally, there are always hordes of sugar-coated, overproduced woman singers. The veteran pop divas are Krisdayanti and Anggun (think Indonesian versions of Mariah Carey or Janet Jackson), still clinging to the upper reaches of the charts even as swarms of younger models rise from below—the likes of Gita Gutawa, and

Above Indonesian diva Anggun onstage.
Above middle Noah—formerly known as Peterpan—in action.

Right Nazril "Ariel" Irham, onstage, before he went to prison!

Bottom Veteran rockers Slank have been going strong for well over three decades. Originally founded by a gaggle of teenage buskers and former Rolling Stones cover artists, they've become genuine superstars, with more than 20 albums to their name.

Cinta Laura. But the ultimate diva is the unstoppable commercial juggernaut that is Agnes Monica.

The other perennial chart fodder comes from quartets of sensitive men with designer tattoos and emotional problems. Many of these soft rock bands—Radja, Ungu, Noah and the like—started out in the underground back in the 1990s, but while they usually proclaim Nirvana amongst their formative influences, to me they tend to sound more like Nickelback on a bad day.

POP FACTORIES

It's no surprise that such a pop-crazed country has embraced the 21st-century reality TV talent show format. All the big international talent show franchises have successful Indonesian versions. First up was an Indonesian spin-off of the New Zealand-forged *Popstars* in 2003, followed in short order by *Akademi Fantasi Indosiar*, based on an original Mexican format. Then in 2004 came the big one—*Indonesian Idol*, a spin-off that massively outstripped the success of the UK original, *Pop Idol*. More recently both *The Voice* and *X Factor* have hit Indonesian screens and have been massive ratings successes.

Iwan Fals

He's Indonesia's answer to Bruce Springsteen—a blue-collar guitar hero with a social conscience, beloved of truck drivers and arts students alike, and still going strong in middle age. Iwan Fals was born in Jakarta in 1961 and he started his musical career not on some TV talent show, but as a street busker. He found commercial success from the early 1980s onwards, with a musical style rooted in acoustic ballads and a rich, gravelly voice which always reminds me of the Irish folk singer Christy Moore.

Iwan Fals is often described as a protest singer, and he often got into trouble with the authoritarian New Order government. But his protest usually comes in the form of observational social commentary, rather than outright attacks—an approach that started with his early hit, the deceptively jaunty tale of an underpaid teacher, *Guru Oemar Bakri*. And while most young pop stars might as well be from another planet, working class people still feel able to identify with Iwan Fals. I once asked a truck driver, who I met at the roadside in East Java, why he and so many other truckers had Iwan Fals stickers plastered to their cabs. He grinned and said proudly, "He's a street kid, like us!"

Agnes Monica Goes Global!

If an Indonesian artist was ever going to make it big internationally it was bound to be Agnes Monica. She's been a relentlessly driven music-making machine since the age of six. In fact, I sometimes wonder if she's actually a nuclear-powered commercial robot created by shadowy marketing executives, rather than a pretty Chinese-Indonesian girl from Jakarta...

Agnes—who rebranded herself as "Agnez Mo" for the American market in 2013—started out as a child star with a string of cutesy novelty albums back in the early 90s, then shifted to acting in soap operas, before exploding onto the domestic pop music scene in 2003 with the album *And the Story Goes*. In no time at all she won every music award going, and scored endless hits. She also embraced the peripheral commercial benefits of the Indonesian music industry with great enthusiasm. Drive through any city in the country and you'll see Agnes beaming from billboards and buses, advertising everything from motorbikes to cold-and-flu remedies. Her greatest hits album, *Agnes Is My Name*, was sold packaged with KFC chicken boxes.

But Agnes has always had her sights set on wider horizons, and in recent years she's been working her socks off to make it in America—which she has now, sort of, done. In 2013 she released the English-language single "Coke Bottle", featuring Timbaland, T.I., and a very sleek video. It was the sort of generic mainstream R&B that goes down well stateside, and though it didn't make it onto the

Agnes in the early days, before she became Agnez.

Billboard charts it did get plenty of airplay. Another successful international single, "Boy Magnet", followed in 2015.

I can't say I'm really a fan of Agnes' music, though I'll admit that she's got some funky moves and an original sense of fashion. But it's impossible not to admire her relentless ambition. I doubt she'll stop until she's conquered the world.

The formats are more or less identical to the international originals—with schadenfreude-laden audition reels, and celebrity "coaches" and judging panels (almost invariably featuring cartoonish veteran rocker-cum-producer Ahmad Dhani, a man who somehow manages to combine reactionary politics and aggressive machismo with a profound love of Freddie Mercury). The talent shows have produced a few chart-toppers, though so far only 2007 *Indonesian Idol* winner Rini Wulandari seems to have had a long-term career.

THE INDIE ALTERNATIVES

Although I'm as susceptible to a catchy pop hook as the next person, I used to think that the Indonesian mainstream didn't have all that much to offer someone like me with more alternative musical inclinations. Sure, a few of the veteran big voices-broken hearts brigade held onto a certain amount of rock cred despite the lapses into balladry—Slank in particular (their foot-stomping 2004 blues-rock critique of modern Indonesian society, *Gossip Jalanan*, is my favorite track). But for the most part I had to look to the underground for my personal Indonesian playlists. But towards the end of the last decade some more original sounds started to pop up on mainstream radio and TV in Indonesia.

There was the high-octane pop-punk of Pee Wee Gaskins, and the hilarious antics of The Changcuters. Emerging from the eminently musical city of Bandung, the fact that The Changcuters took their name from a slang term for underpants tells you that they were worlds apart from the usual very serious stuff of Indonesian pop. They were flat-out hilarious, with silly lyrics and sillier clothes, but their Britpop-flavored music was great, especially their Stones-inspired megahit *I Love you Bibeh*.

Since then there seems to have been a bit more color in the Indonesian charts. And, propelled by the social media revolution, genuinely innovative indie bands poke their heads into the mainstream from time to time—from the Jakarta hipsters Hightime Rebellion (who sound like a very cool cross between seminal Swedish punks Refused and Icelandic folk-rockers Of Monsters and Men), to flower-powered, Celtic-tinged Deugalih and Folks. Musically speaking Indonesia is, as always, a very exciting place to be.

Indonesian Jazz:
An Interview with Terry Collins

Indonesia has a vast and vibrant jazz scene, with some genuinely out-there fusion and prog-rock elements at the fringes. There are annual jazz festivals in most major cities. Indonesia has thrown up a few internationally renowned jazz musicians over the years too, most recently pianist Joey Alexander who burst onto the world stage in 2015 with a bestselling album and two Grammy nominations—and all at the tender age of eleven!

The writer and long-term Jakarta resident Terry Collins knows a thing or two about Indonesian jazz. He's been documenting the scene and exploring its history for years, and together with fellow jazz-loving expat Arlo Hennings he created Indojazzia.net. I caught up with Terry to get some insights on jazz past, present, and future.

Where and when did Indonesia's jazz scene start?

The first "jazz era" started in 1919 in Batavia [modern Jakarta]. A San Francisco-based Boys Club brought 42 boys who provided an eclectic program of entertainment, with jazz accompaniment. This inspired high school students to form jazz bands with a repertoire from American films, 78rpm discs, and sheet music.

The jazz played post-independence was mainly Indonesian songs, some purely instrumental, with generic mambo and cha-cha rhythms. The first ethno-jazz album of note, *Djanger Bali*, was recorded following an appearance at the Berlin Jazz Festival in 1967 by the Indonesian All-Stars, featuring guitarist Jack Lemmers (Lesmana) and Bubi Chen.

In 1977 Guruh Sukanoputra, Sukarno's son, recruited prog-rock group Guru to record *Guruh Gypsy*, a fusion of prog-rock and gamelan. The next significant development happened in the early 90s when three groups, Karimata, Krakatau, and Java Jazz, released ethno-jazz albums.

Can you sum up the current Indonesian jazz scene in a nutshell?

There are still generational links to the pioneering maestros of the 60s and seventies, so "standards" are often heard. It's only since the abdication of the dictator Suharto that artists have felt free to explore their own creative muses. Jazz doesn't afford financial security, so many musicians teach privately or in music schools or, as in the case of a truly original guitarist, Tohpati, through sessions.

Are there any bands or artists who bring a specifically and uniquely Indonesian fusion element?

Good jazz comes from the heart, so most have an echo of their ethnic heritage in their music, but some are more overt than others: Riza Arshad's simakDialog has Sundanese percussion; guitarist Dewa Budjana's compositions reflect his Balinese Hinduism; pianist Sri Hanuraga takes "traditional" Indonesian songs way beyond their borders; and Dwiki Dharmawan incorporates Sundanese percussion and other traditional sounds in his various groups.

Who are your personal favorite artists?

Ligro, IKYWMC, Tuslah, Tomorrow Peoples Ensemble because they are playing music which is unlike anything heard anywhere else. And I would give a special heads up to Sri Hanuraga who has studied jazz abroad and has "channeled" Errol Garner for me.

Can you tell us something about the IndoJazzia project?

IndoJazzia.net was set up to promote Indonesian jazz worldwide through the sharing of information and resources. We are particularly interested in younger musicians, such as I Know You Well Miss Clara from Yogyakarta, who are totally unique and are now under our managerial wing. We are moving towards having a record label to distribute albums which have been overlooked yet have a historical interest. We are also researching *A History of Jazz in Indonesia* because that is the foundation for the present, and the future.

www.indojazzia.net

The annual Java Jazz festival features dozens of local and international acts on multiple stages in a Jakarta convention complex.

THE INDONESIAN PUNK SCENE

Forget dangdut. Forget gamelan orchestras and kroncong ensembles. And definitely forget Agnes Monica. The true musical spirit of Indonesia is punk rock. That might seem an odd thing to say, but Indonesia is home to what is almost certainly the biggest underground punk scene on the planet. And what's more, while naysayers have been proclaiming the death of punk in Britain and America pretty much from the moment the genre first raised its spiky head, declaring it moribund or bemoaning its commercialization, the Indonesian scene is both spectacularly vibrant and utterly rooted in gritty, DIY authenticity. Welcome to the Punk Archipelago.

Sumatran punkers.

Most people agree that what lit the fuse for Indonesia's punk rock explosion was the sudden commercial success of American pop-punk—and in particular Green Day—in the mid-1990s (a moment which also introduced this then teenage Cornish surfer kid, bored with the gloomy navel-gazing of grunge, to the joys of punk rock). There's a certain irony here: it was the grand corporatization of American punk, the moment of ultimate selling out, which kick-started an Indonesian scene with serious underground cred.

There had, of course, been a few Indonesian punkers before the mid-90s, inspired by the Sex Pistols and the Ramones. But they had been little more than misfits on the edge of the Jakarta heavy metal scene (which is also still vibrant today, though it definitely plays second fiddle to punk in the Indonesian underground). What gave the nascent punk rock revolution such drive was the political context. By the time Green Day stopped by in Jakarta on their world tour in 1996, Suharto's authoritarian New Order regime was beginning to totter, and Indonesia's student and youth movements were beginning to find their political voice for the first time in decades. And in grimy back alleys and suburban boarding houses across the country, politically engaged punk bands were coming into being.

What made punk so special in Indonesia was that, unlike other musical scenes that took their initial inspiration from overseas, it was not the preserve of the middle classes. It was a thing of the streets; it belonged to the working classes, and they made it their own. And the live punk shows that you'll find in grimy underground clubs from Surabaya to Medan still feel wildly—and at times a little scarily—authentic compared to the sanitized stadium gigs in Britain and America.

Right Street punks in Sumatra.

Far right Celtic punks The Cloves and the Tobacco.

Superman is Dead

The first Indonesian music I ever heard was a dodgy, home-copied cassette of a band called Superman is Dead. Two decades later they're still going strong, and these days they're proper punk rock royalty.

Superman is Dead (SID for short) formed in Kuta, Bali's biggest tourist resort, way back in 1995. This might not make much sense if your idea of punk origins involves grimy New York basements or grim postindustrial England. But 1995 was a high water mark in the global explosion of sunny Californian skate-punk—and Kuta is about as close to Orange County as it gets in Indonesia. Guitarist and front-man Bobby Kool, bassist Eka Rock, and drummer Jerinx took the Californian sound of NOFX, Green Day, No Use for a Name, and Lagwagon, threw in a hint of punk'n'roll, and made it their own.

The fact that Indonesia's most successful punk band is not from Jakarta or Bandung, but from Bali is a strange state of affairs, and SID have occasionally had a hard time from the scene hardliners. There were bizarre rumors for a while that Jerinx had an secret tattoo expressing anti-Java sentiments, and like many a punk band before them they got a barrage of condemnation from the underground purists when they signed with major label, Sony Music Indonesia, in 2003. But as far as I'm concerned they've made a great job of keeping it real. Their major label debut, *Kuta Rock City*, is one of the best punk albums to emerge from Indonesia, and in the face of label pressure they still record a good proportion of their songs in English—regarded as bad commercial practice in the domestic music industry.

They played the Warped Tour in America way back in 2009 (in your face, Agnes Monica!), and supported NOFX on their visits to Indonesia. For sure, their more recent albums have piled a bit more weight on the pop side of the pop-punk scales, with polished tracks of the kind your mum could hum along to, but they've still got serious punk rock cred for their committed involvement with environmental activism in Bali. And if you happen to be in Bali yourself, go to Kuta, turn off the Jalan Legian main drag and head down the narrow street known as Poppies II. After a couple of hundred yards you'll spot a dark doorway into a place called the Twice Bar. It's owned by drummer Jerinx, and here amidst the tourist mayhem, you'll find the hub of Bali's punk scene. If you're lucky, SID themselves might even be at home...

The Aceh 64

In late 2011 Indonesia's punk scene hit the international headlines. In Banda Aceh—capital of the once restive province at the northern tip of Sumatra—64 street punks were rounded up by local police at an open air punk show, and forced into a moral reeducation program, their mohawks shaved off and their leather jackets burnt. For a while "the Aceh 64" became an international cause célèbre, and foreign journalists portrayed the incident as a clash between punk and Islam (notoriously conservative Aceh is the one part of Indonesia where Islamic Sharia underpins local bylaws). But when Aceh's deputy governor called punk "a social disease", she wasn't expressing an opinion rooted in fundamentalist Islam; she was voicing the view of mainstream secular Indonesian society far beyond Aceh. Tattooed, poor, and distinctly different, street punks are viewed as a suspect "other" by polite society wherever they exist. Religion doesn't really have anything to do with it, and many Indonesian punks are proudly practicing Muslims. In fact, there's even a "One Finger Movement", a subset of devout Muslim punks equivalent to the fundamentalist Christian straight edge bands in America.

PUNK ROCK ARCHIPELAGO

Without a doubt, the best known Indonesian punk band is Bali's Superman is Dead—SID for short—with their catchy, Green Day-inspired pop-punk. Inevitably, the underground purists think that SID, who are signed to major label Sony Music Indonesia, are sellouts—an accusation also sometimes leveled at their fellow pop-punk veterans, the Bandung-based Rocket Rockers. But these bands are the tip of the iceberg, and just beneath the surface you'll find hordes of old-school purists, taking their stylistic and musical inspiration from the Exploited, Black Flag and the Ramones, rather than Blink 182 and Sum 41.

One of the original Jakarta punk bands was the frenetic, Ramones-style Antiseptic. They no longer exist, but plenty of other veterans are still going strong, not least the superfast, super-shouty Turtles Jr, who have been rocking hard since 1992, and Jeruji, a machine gun-paced hardcore band from the eternal musical wellspring of Bandung. And there are always new bands popping up—from fierce all-girl Jollyty Joy to raging all-boy hardcore band Bocor 13.

Perhaps the most unexpected facet of the Indonesian punk scene is the wealth of Celtic folk punk. That's right—if you want to find the greatest concentration of Guinness-swilling, fiddle-playing, shamrock-toting, Flogging Molly-style bands in the world, you won't find it in Boston, and you definitely won't find it in Dublin. You'll need to head to Indonesia. There are dozens of Celtic punk bands—from Yogyakarta's Dirty Glass to Semarang's Billy the Kid, and from Forgotten Generation (who sound like a better version of Swingin' Utters) to The Working Class Symphony (who have a fine line in Iwan Fals-style acoustic balladry to offset their faster tracks). My personal favorites, however, are The Cloves and the Tobacco (the name is a reference to Indonesian *kretek* cigarettes) who are better than the Dropkick Murphys. Seriously.

PUNK AND POLITICS

Punk's supposedly radical stance might have long since become a joke in the West, amidst the movie soundtracks and the corporate sponsorship. But Indonesia's punk scene was forged in the ferment of a real revolution—the protest movement that toppled Suharto in the 1990s. The scene still has a powerful political pulse, never better demonstrated than by the mighty Marjinal, whose members were at the forefront of the anti-Suharto movement.

Marjinal are, in my opinion, one of the very best Indonesian punk bands. They also look spectacularly cool—like hungry road warriors straight out of a *Mad Max* movie. But most importantly of all they have a real social conscience. The band is based in a down-at-heel neighborhood of South Jakarta, and they head a punk collective called *Taring Babi* ("Pig's Fang"), which runs art workshops, teaches street kids how to play the ukulele, and works on self-help projects with working class communities—the DIY punk ethos expanded beyond music to offer empowerment to the poorest sections of society.

A Punk Rock Playlist

Marjinal, *Negri Ngeri* This raging anthem of discontent is Marjinal's best-known track.

Forgotten Generation, *Ingkar* A song to raise a glass to, and a prime example of Indonesian Celtic punk.

Turtles Jr., *Anjing Goblok Tai Babi* One blistering minute of foul-mouthed fury from the veteran hardcore band.

The Cloves and the Tobacco, *The Indian Ocean* The sound might be more North Atlantic than Indian Ocean, but this is top-notch Indo Celtic punk.

Superman is Dead, *Kuta Rock City* English-language pop-punk classic from the Bali boys.

SOUNDS OF THE STREET:
A THRIVING BUSKER CULTURE

At every bus terminal, every night market, and every traffic intersection you'll find them: lean young men—and occasionally women—in torn jeans toting acoustic guitars. They are the foot soldiers in Indonesia's musical army.

On the one hand the legions of pengamen ("buskers") are simply a sad manifestation of poverty. But in Indonesian popular consciousness, there's a hint of rugged romance in the vision of a ragged troubadour, living by his wits, master to no man, and wielding a guitar like the sword of an old-time rebel prince. And perhaps most importantly, many Indonesian buskers are seriously talented.

Indonesian buskers seem to come in three main varieties. There are the musical beggars—many of them tiny children—who haunt busy intersections and weave their way through the stalled traffic strumming wrecked ukuleles for coins. Whether or not these poor kids can play doesn't really matter, but there's another type of busker for whom a wanton lack of ability is actually an advantage. These willfully tuneless balladeers target pavement cafés. They enter, and move from table to table singing horribly. The object is to get each customer to hand over a few coins as quickly as possible simply to get them to go away. It's a sort of musical extortion, and they usually work with a sort of joyless, fast-moving professionalism. But the real kings of the streets—and the ones who often

have real talent—are the buskers who work the buses. Sometimes they work alone; sometimes in pairs; and sometimes as full ensembles, with multiple instruments.

Many of these top-level pengamen show a genuine commitment to their music, and their self-penned songs are often as good as anything in the charts. And there is always the elusive chance of a busker hitting the big time. The mighty Iwan Fals started out playing on the streets, as did the veteran bluesrockers Slank, and in 2008 a Jakarta busker, Januarisman, actually won *Indonesian Idol*.

Above and left Some of Jakarta's street buskers are seriously talented. Some stick to one spot; some are always on the move, shifting between street and café locations.

A Moving Portrait of Buskers' Lives

Buskers have always belonged to the margins of Indonesian society, the sort of people whose stories are seldom told. But a beautiful 2012 documentary by Canadian-born, Jakarta-based writer and filmmaker Daniel Ziv brought the lives of three of their number into focus. *Jalanan* was filmed over four and a half years, and it follows the lives of three talented buskers, Boni, Ho, and Titi. The film—which found great acclaim on the international festival circuit, and prompted plenty of debate in Indonesia—is both an intimate portrait of the three protagonists, and a searching look through the cracks in Indonesia's glittering developmental façade.

Tak Gendong! A Ringtone Megahit

If an Indonesian busker finds fame, it's generally safe to assume that it'll be one of the ones who can actually sing. But not always. In 2009 a dreadlocked 60-year-old by the name of Mbah Surip because an instant celebrity when his comedy reggae track *Tak Gendong* ("I'll carry you") became a viral ringtone megahit. Safe to say, Mbah Surip—who had started his musical career busking on Jakarta buses—was no Bob Marley, but the song earned him Rp4.5 billion in royalties from the mobile phone operator. Sadly he didn't have long to enjoy it. He died of a heart attack just a few months after hitting the big time.

CHAPTER 4

CINEMA, TV AND MEDIA

Looking for some cheap cinematic thrills courtesy of a B-movie encounter with a *kuntilanak*? Want to know what makes a successful *sinetron*, or understand why mixed-race Indonesians are shoo-ins for onscreen celebrity? Or maybe you'd rather check out the scandals in the Jakarta gutter press, or strike a literary pose with the sharpest modern novelists? It's time to explore the world of Indonesian cinema, media, and literature.

TROPICAL CELLULOID DREAMS: A HISTORY OF INDONESIAN CINEMA

Cloying teen romances, either with or without a side order of religious piety; the occasional earnest historical biopic with political sentiments stuck in 1945; and a whole bunch of low-budget sexy vampire-zombies... A first glance at the standard output of the mainstream Indonesian film industry doesn't look too promising. But scratch the surface and you'll find some increasingly sophisticated indie storytelling. Even the perennial horror genre has had an upgrade in recent years. Meanwhile, thanks to an unlikely creative collaboration between a transplanted Welshman and a Jakarta martial arts genius, Indonesia has also spawned arguably the most stylish onscreen violence since the death of Bruce Lee...

CINEMATIC HISTORY

Indonesian cinema has old and deep roots, stretching way back to the 1920s, when a handful of Dutch and Chinese-Indonesian producers started turning out locally made movies for screening in the theaters of the colonial cities of Java and Sumatra. The first movie ever shot in Indonesia was *Loetoeng Kasaroeng*, a Sundanese folktale released way back in 1926. Plot details are sketchy, for this is one of those ghostly "lost films", of which no copy survives.

Above *Ada Apa Dengan Cinta?* ("What's up with Love?")—the ultimate teen romance blockbuster.

Left Indonesia's first movie, 1926's *Loetoeng Kasaroeng.*

A proper Indonesian film industry—based mainly in Jakarta—didn't really have a chance to develop until after the country had won its independence. As with the popular music industry, official hostility to cultural imports actually gave local creatives an extra imperative: few Hollywood movies made it past the censors. By the 1980s, with the Indonesian economy booming but with the authorities still keeping their censorious eye on foreign films, the local industry had some 2,800 movie theaters nationwide to supply, and significant resources with which to do the job. Many industry insiders still look back on the well-funded 1980s as the golden age of Indonesian cinema. Production values were certainly decent, but filmmakers still had to run the censors' gauntlet, and the 1980s stuff that you'll occasionally see on TV isn't exactly edgy.

In the 1990s the restrictions on imported films from Hollywood, Bollywood, and Hong Kong were largely lifted, just as pirate videos and near-universal TV ownership were cutting swaths through the old-fashioned small-town theaters (even today, with new multiplexes opening in city malls, the number of cinemas nationwide is only a third of what it was in the 1980s). The Indonesian film industry, to be blunt, went to the dogs, retreating to its core of trashy low-budget horror and what were basically feature-length *sinetron* episodes. But since the start of the new century the gloss has crept back into the mainstream, while on the indie side of the screen there have been sophisticated stirrings.

TEEN ROMANCE AND HORROR

They're the two eternal fallback forms in Indonesian cinema: boy-meets-girl in a middle-class senior high school setting; and a supernatural creature is borrowed from folklore, given a faintly pornographic makeover, and set to rampage in a graveyard with lashings of dry ice. The first genre has been around for a long time, but the seminal example in modern cinema is 2002's *Ada Apa Dengan Cinta?* (The name

Gareth Evans

Jakarta's Greatest Welsh Director

In 2011 Indonesia scored its first international box office hit. Called *The Raid: Redemption* (released as *Serbuan Maut*, "Deadly Raid", in Indonesia), it was an eye-popping fiesta of martial arts mayhem, featuring good and bad cops fighting their way up the levels of a hellish tower block full of very wicked people. The star was a young *pencak silat* maestro named Iko Uwais. And the director, bizarrely, was a guy called Gareth Evans who hailed from the Welsh valleys. Uwais and Evans met when the Welshman was working on a documentary about pencak silat after moving to Jakarta with his Indonesian wife. The pair went on to collaborate on a feature film, *Merantau*, which gathered a cult following for Evans' snappy directing style and Uwais' brutally stylish moves. Then came *The Raid*, followed by *The Raid II*. Since then Evans has been linked to all sorts of Hollywood projects; *The Raid III* is in the pipeline, and Iko Uwais even ended up with a part in *Star Wars: The Force Awakens*.

means "What's up with Love?" which is a pun: the main female character is called Cinta, "Love".) Starring Dian Sastrowardoyo and Nicholas Saputra (who are pretty much essential fixtures in this sort of film) in a pretty conventional high school-set friendship-and-romance saga, it was a nationwide megahit, and it set the standard for the genre in the years to come. There have been endless cookie-cutter variations on the same kind of theme—including a distinct subgenre imbued with wholesome Islamic values, most notably 2008's *Ayat-Ayat Cinta* ("The Verses of Love").

There's nothing remotely wholesome or Islamic about the other Indonesian cinema staple, however. The Indonesian film industry churns out horror movies on bargain-basement budgets, and rarely seems willing to splash out on such

Romance gets an indie spin in *Tiga Hari Untuk Selamanya* (Three Days for Eternity).

nonessential elements as proper scripts. Horrors invariably feature one of three ghost-zombie species: *kuntilanak*, *pocong*, or the silliest of all Indonesian ghosts, the "crawling nurse", *suster ngesot*, generally played by some raunchy dangdut singer.

Tjoet Nja' Dhien

The film that's usually dubbed the ultimate Indonesian "classic" is the 1988 historical epic, Tjoet Nja' Dhien, starring Christine Hakim as a real-life female Acehnese guerilla leader, battling brutal colonial Dutch forces at the turn of the 20th century. It was made in the big-budget days of the 1980s, and it's lavishly realized and earnestly acted—a sort of Indonesian *Lawrence of Arabia* or *Gandhi*. It won the Best International Film at the 1989 Cannes Film Festival.

Indonesia as Depicted in **Western Films**

Without a shadow of a doubt, the Indonesia-set film that's had the most international impact in recent years was a 2012 documentary called *The Act of Killing*. The British-American filmmaker Joshua Oppenheimer spent years in northern Sumatra, quietly examining the social legacy of the terrible anti-communist massacres of the mid-1960s. His approach was far from conventional (he focused on the perpetrators rather than the victims), and the result is one of the most disturbing insights into the dark side of humanity that you'll ever see—with the impact only heightened by moments of striking filmic beauty. Oppenheimer returned in 2014 with a follow-up, The *Look of Silence*, which took a quieter approach and brought the focus back to the victims, with similarly devastating effect. Foreign critics and festival juries generally threw themselves into paroxysms of delight over Oppenheimer's work, though there were occasional dissenting voices from amongst scholars of Indonesian history. It's certainly true that you'll learn absolutely nothing about the historical context of the killings from these movies, but their terrible and beautiful power is undeniable.

Generally, however, when foreign filmmakers descend on Indonesia, the results are pretty shoddy. You can be pretty much guaranteed a whole bunch of tacky tropical clichés and plenty of wild inaccuracy in the portrayal of the country and its people—a theme that began in 1969 with *Krakatoa*, *East of Java*, a trashy disaster movie that relocated the famous volcano at the wrong end of Java (it really lies to the west), and that was filmed nowhere near Indonesia. Prime recent examples have included *Eat Pray Love*, in which Julia Roberts indulges her ego and ignores the locals in an airbrushed version of Bali, and a 2013 action movie called *Java Heat*. It featured evil terrorist Mickey Rourke kidnapping the "Sultana of Java". If you've never heard of it, count yourself lucky. The one Indonesia-set Hollywood film that's actually worth watching is the 1982 classic, *The Year of Living Dangerously*, set against the backdrop of Sukarno's final months in office. The locals don't get much of a look, and it was actually filmed in the Philippines, but it's thoroughly atmospheric—and Mel Gibson, Linda Hunt and Sigourney Weaver are all brilliant in the main roles.

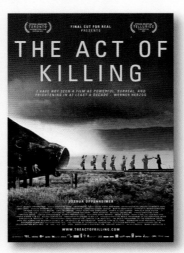

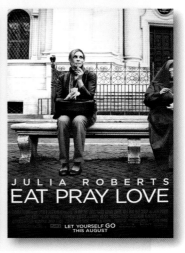

THE INDIE UPSWING

In the last decade a new generation of Jakarta-based directors has started to shake up the Indonesian cinema scene. Films like 2008's bittersweet road movie *Tiga Hari Untuk Selamanya* (*Three Days for Eternity*) have brought an indie sensibility and a new frankness about sex to the romance format, and the creepy *Belenggu* (*Shackle*) in 2012 freshened up the horror format: suffice to say it featured a sinister giant rabbit a la *Donnie Darko*, and no sexy dangdut singers…

Probably the most versatile and creative of the new generation of Indonesian filmmakers is Joko Anwar, a former journalist turned scriptwriter turned director. His writing and directing portfolio includes everything from quirky romantic comedy (*Janji Joni*, *Joni's Promise*) to thoroughly weird noir (*Kala*), and genuinely disturbing psychological horror (*Pintu Terlarang*, *The Forbidden Door*). In a sure sign of the new, self-fertilizing creative fizz in the Indonesian film scene, Anwar's 2015 experiment with social realism, *A Copy of My Mind*, seemed to take its stylistic cue from the gritty, groundbreaking documentaries that have recently emerged from Indonesia. Edgier still is director Lucky Kuswandi—ever wanted to see a film about a transsexual superhero? Well Kuswandi's made one; it's called *Madame X*, and while it's gloriously silly it's also radical. There is definitely plenty going on in Indonesian cinema these days.

CHANNEL SURFING:
THE INDONESIAN TUBE

A cool blue glow pervades communal spaces in every corner of Indonesia, from mountain villages in Sumatra, to harbor towns in Maluku. Indonesia is a true TV nation, and even in the age of the Internet, television still has an enormous reach, with an estimated 90 percent rate of penetration in the national population. As far as its fans are concerned it's been an important tool in binding a vast and disparate country together. Critics, meanwhile, condemn it as a means of propagating Jakarta-Java cultural hegemony and rotting the brains of the nation with a diet of vulgar entertainment and trashy soap operas. But whatever you think, even if you don't speak Indonesian, it can be a lot of fun to watch—for about five minutes, anyway…

TV has become the universal babysitter in Indonesian homes, as elsewhere.

State-run TVRI is the granddaddy of Indonesian television stations, and it's been broadcasting since the early 1960s. During Suharto's New Order rule, the authorities kept a tight grip on public broadcasters, and there were only a handful of lackluster channels. But since the turn of the 21st century, deregulation has brought a wide array of commercial terrestrial and satellite TV stations. TVRI is still going, but it has to fight for viewers with RCTI, MNCTV, Trans 7, Trans TV, and more.

If you're expecting edifying public broadcasting in Indonesia, you might be a little disappointed. TV here is dominated by mass-appeal commercialism, with a lot of talent shows, low-brow comedy, tacky talk shows, and above all, soap operas. There is also lots of news programing, but it tends to lean towards the sensationalist (to the extent of adding dramatic background music to reports of accidents and disasters). There's also a lot of advertising, and one of the most striking things is that the production values of the ads often far outstrip those of the shows themselves. Tobacco companies and noodle manufacturers routinely serve up lavishly filmed and artfully directed visions in the ad breaks between soap operas which look like they've been shot on a camera phone! In fact, instant noodle-maker Indomie's classic *Satu Selera* ad—a rousing, multilingual, one-nation musical number—is one of the best things I've ever seen on TV in Indonesia!

THE WONDERS OF SINETRON

If you've ever watched even a few minutes of Indonesian television, chances are you'll have seen something like this: a masterclass of horrendous overacting, filmed in a very upscale suburban house with terrible lighting and appalling acoustics, in which people wearing far too much make up were unconvincingly shouting at each other, and which ended up with someone getting slapped, someone in floods

Above and right In the name of cross-cultural understanding, a diplomat from the US embassy in Jakarta gets a walk-on role in *Tukang Bubur Naik Haji* (*The Rice-Porridge Seller Goes on the Haj*), a long-running sinetron religi.

Opera Van Java: How Messing Around with Traditional Theater Arts Created a Broadcast Behemoth

In 2008 the Trans7 channel launched a new show, based on the *wayang wong*, the traditional Javanese dance format which tells stylized tales from the Indian epics the *Ramayana* and *Mahabharata*. It came with a full gamelan accompaniment and a *dalang*—a master of ceremonies to direct the performance. But if serious aficionados were hoping it might bring some sophisticated refinement to the evening schedules, they were sorely disappointed, for the show named *Opera Van Java* took some serious liberties. It was basically a comedy improvisation show, in which the main cast—Andre Taulany, Nunung, Azis Gagap, and supreme clown Sule—acted out sketches, some based on folklore and mythology, some in silly modern scenarios, at the behest of *dalang* Parto, with the orchestra sporadically bursting into gamelan covers of pop songs. Its real appeal, though, lay in its sheer anarchy, with the cast continuously corpsing, destroying the polystyrene props, and generally behaving like idiots. And it was a huge hit, running five nights a week at its peak, attracting enormous audiences, and even generating a nationwide roadshow. The run ended in 2014, and though there have been various subsequent spin-offs, it's left a very big hole in the schedule.

of hysterical tears, or someone fainting. What you saw was a *sinetron*…

Sinetron—the name is short for *sinema elekronik*, soap operas or telenovelas by any other name—are Indonesia's dominant televisual phenomenon. There are dozens of them—from one-season wonders to ongoing epics that have long since passed the thousand-episode mark. Indonesians love to mock them, laugh at the bad acting, the shoddy production values, and the ridiculous clichés (there's always a wicked stepmother or an evil sister-in-law, and there's always a hilariously unconvincing traffic accident). But they also love to watch them.

The sinetron phenomenon is often credited to one man, Surabaya-born Indian-Indonesian producer Raam Punjabi. He started out working in cinema,

but when the Indonesian film industry hit the buffers at the start of the 1990s he turned his attention to TV, picked up on the existing Indonesian fondness for imported Latin-American and Indian soaps, and presided over a sinetron explosion. He's still at it, and his nephew Manoj Punjabi is also now one of Indonesia's biggest sinetron producers.

The classic sinetron storyline is a convoluted family saga, set amongst luxury housing developments and exclusive private hospitals. But there are also comedy sinetron such as *Suami Suami Takut Istri* ("Husbands who are Scared of their Wives") and supernatural sinetron—which generally feature ghosts with subtler makeup than the wicked stepmothers in the regular sinetron. And since the late 1990s there has also been a glut of *sinetron religi*—religious sinetron, which to a cynic might look like any other sinetron, just with added Muslim skullcaps and headscarves, but which in some cases, such as the output of the Citra Sinema production company, do attempt to offer a serious moral message. Short-running sinetron religi have become an essential part of the Ramadan scheduling each year, but there are others that play week after week, all year round, such as *Tukang Bubur Naik Haji* ("The Rice-Porridge Seller Goes on the Haj") which finally ended in 2017 after 2,185 episodes.

THE CELEBRITY ETHNICITY
If an Indonesian goes on so much as a single date with a Caucasian, certain friends and aunties will probably start speculating about the future careers of their unborn offspring: "They'll be celebrities!" Because if you want to have a successful television or cinema career in Indonesia, the single best thing you can do is to be born mixed race…

"Indos"—people of Eurasian descent—have been around in Indonesia since a few years after the first Portuguese sailors arrived in the 1500s. They've played many roles over the centuries, but since the 1980s, as far as the Indonesian general public is concerned, they've been born for just one purpose: to be famous. Can't sing? Can't act? Can't even speak Indonesian? It doesn't matter if you're visibly of mixed race.

Politician Marty Natalegawa gets a grilling from the news crews.

Below At the heart of the action—an RCTI news crew on location in Jakarta.

Three of Indonesia's multitude of mixed-race celebs—Julie Estelle (**top left**), Dewi Sandra (**above**) and Christian Sugiono (**left**).

Indos account for a miniscule fraction of the Indonesian population, but they are massively disproportionately represented in the casts of films and sinetron, in modelling, and in the mainstream music industry. And many famous Indos seem to serve as all-round celebrities, doing a bit of acting, a bit of presenting, a bit of singing, and a whole lot of look-ing Indo. Luna Maya, Nicholas Saputra, Dewi Sandra, Rianti Cartwright, Carissa Putri, Cinta Laura—these are just a few of Indonesia's many mixed-race celebs.

Conventional wisdom has it that Indos are simply more likely to match up to traditional Indonesian ideals of beauty, with fairer skin, rounder eyes, and longer, straighter noses—and critics point out that the dominance of such looks onscreen helps further the power-ful message of a cosmetics industry where "skin whitening" is the dominant product property, and where some girls feel compelled to undergo surgery to change the shape of their eyes and nose. On the other side, meanwhile, some young Indos complain that societal presumptions that they're bound for stardom can make it hard to be taken seriously or to follow other, less glamor-ous career paths.

Chat Show Kings

Indonesia loves a TV chat show, and it has a trio of diverse personalities, vying for the title of king of the onscreen sofa. MetroTV weighs in with Andy Noya and his long-running *Kick Andy* (no kick-ing involved) show in the Friday night primetime slot. Andy (who used to sport an afro but who's now completely bald) is decidedly nice, and his show is thoroughly wholesome—lots of local heroes, teenage geniuses, and housewives with tales of "journeys back to life" after tragedy. He's basically a bald, male Oprah Winfrey.

Over on Trans7, and in an appropri-ately later slot, you'll find a non-bald and not-so-nice comedian by the name of Tukul Arwana. Tukul's presenting style generally lurches in the direction of off-color slapstick, with lots of mug-ging for the faintly hysterical audience and a tendency for eyebrow-raising in-nuendo. His original show, *Empat Mata* ("Four Eyes"), was actually banned by the Indonesian Broadcasting Commis-sion in 2008 after he made a guest eat a live goldfish on air, though it seam-lessly morphed into *Bukan Empat Mata* ("Not Four Eyes") which has also had a fair bit of censure for "vulgarity".

Trans7 is also home to another, much more interesting chat show host: one Deddy Corbuzier, with *Hitam Putih* ("Black and White"). He happens to be another completely bald man, but unlike cuddly Andy Noya, he has a genuine air of slightly threatening cool—aided by his ten-dency to wear eyeliner and the fact that he's also a professional magi-cian and mentalist. He's a good deal more sophisticated than Tukul too...

A BROADSHEET FREE-FOR-ALL: THE INDONESIAN PRESS PACK

Indonesia's print media is one of the biggest and most boisterous—and occasionally most shameless—in the world. Go into any train station in the country and check out the newsstands. There are dozens upon dozens of daily papers, news weeklies, and glossy magazines, even in this age of free online content. And while Indonesia has a reputation as a country where very few people read books, people definitely read newspapers. From becak drivers to businessmen, pretty much everyone comes into contact with newsprint at some point in their day.

The Indonesian press has a peculiar status in popular consciousness. On the one hand Indonesian journalists—like journalists the world over—cop flak for being sleazy, exploitative, and untrustworthy. But on the other hand, journalism has historically had a much closer relationship with high literature in Indonesia than in other countries, and the Indonesian press certainly earnt its stripes during the country's struggle for independence. Say the word *wartawan* ("journalist") to an Indonesian, and depending what sort of mood he's in, he might think of a nasty, chain-smoking liar with a pocket full of cash-stuffed envelopes, or he might conjure up a romantic image of a fearless revolutionary poet!

Right A newspaper-seller takes time out to read his wares.
Right above Catching up with the latest news in Yogyakarta.

The press has often had a troubled relationship with authority, and after Suharto came to power in the 1960s, the print media was kept under close scrutiny. Any inclination to go off-message tended to be rewarded with a revoked publishing license. When Suharto fell in the late 1990s, however, virtually all restrictions were lifted, and Indonesia went completely newspaper-crazy. People seemed to be launching newspapers from bedrooms and coffee stalls. By the turn of the 21st century there were around a thousand papers in circulation. Inevitably, many failed to stay the course, but there are still about 170 dailies in print today, and a further 400-odd non-dailies. Most of these papers are local affairs. But there are some big titles with nationwide reach, including *Jawa Pos*, *Media Indonesia*, and *Republika*.

Like every country, Indonesia has its heavyweight broadsheets—the sort of paper that educated, worldly folks like to be seen reading in coffee shops. *Kompas* is probably the classic paper of this type. And like every country, Indonesia has its filthy gutter press—the sort of paper that fixates on crime and scandal, with Jakarta's *Pos Kota* being the archetype. Unlike in Britain and America, the term "tabloid" in Indonesia doesn't have a low-press association. Indonesian tabloids are simply weekly, tabloid-sized publications, usually focusing on a specialist subject—anything from women's issues to railways. There are also weekly news magazines—with *Tempo* best known amongst them, not least for its honorable tussles with authority during the New Order years—plus a huge array of glossy periodicals of every stripe, including Indonesian-language editions of international giants like *Cosmopolitan* and *National Geographic*.

BAD NEWS: THE GUTTER PRESS
I love the sheer vibrancy of Indonesia's print media, and in an era of globally plummeting circulations, I love the fact that it still has a strong pulse. But I do occasionally find myself taken aback by its excesses. For a start, even the most respectable broadsheets routinely print graphic images of murder victims that would never appear without pixels in even the trashiest of British tabloids. And accuracy sometimes leaves a fair bit to be desired—as I know from personal experience.

Read all about it! Surabaya street kids selling newspapers to motorists at traffic lights is still a common sight.

Above Launching a new airline service.

Newspaper photo-editors in regional cities like nothing better than the chance to stick an eye-catching image of a foreigner on the front page. When I was teaching in Surabaya I sometimes had to go to public events—education fairs, English-language speech contests, that sort of thing. At these events, a press photographer would always pop up and snap me, and quite often these pics ended up in the papers the next day— usually with a story attached in which my name was spelt incorrectly, and in which invented quotes were attributed to me, despite the fact I'd never spoken to the reporter!

And then there's corruption. The dark practice of "envelope journalism", in which politicians or businessmen hand reporters cash-stuffed envelopes to ensure favorable coverage, is much discussed in Indonesia. To be fair, the most reputable papers and the best journalists do take serious stands against this sort of thing, but even they are subjected to a sort of low-level bribing every time they go to a press conference. In the UK you won't get so much as a glass of water as a journalist at a press conference. But in Indonesia, you'll get at the very least a packed lunch, and in all likelihood a full-blown goody bag. I once went to a press conference in Jakarta for the launch of a sex education program. It was sponsored by a condom producer, and the goody bags were packed with condom-themed tee shirts, condom-shaped lollipops, condom-based gifts.

News on the go—a hawker selling papers on a Jakarta commuter train.

And actual condoms. I'd gone to the event with another foreign journalist, and we both went home with about five of these bags each—they'd been abandoned by the horribly embarrassed young women who dominate the Jakarta junior press circuit!

Indonesia's English-Language Media

I worked for several years in the English-language arm of Indonesia's print media—copy-editing for a Bali weekly, and freelancing for all sorts of other newspapers and magazines— and I've seen a whole bunch of publications come and go in this strange sector. When it comes to newspapers, the long-running *Jakarta Post* still dominates, though its upstart rival *Jakarta Globe* still has decent online coverage. These papers are rooted in the expat readership in Jakarta, which is also served by various lifestyle magazines, while the very differently complexioned expat and tourist scene in Bali has its own library of monthly glossies to choose from. But there are also a good few glossy periodicals, published in English, but aimed at Indonesians rather than expats—things like *Indonesian Tatler*, and a host of travel, design and lifestyle mags. It might seem strange that any publisher would want to put out an English title in a country where relatively few people speak English, but take a look at the adverts in these magazines and you'll understand: if you publish in English you can assure your advertisers that your readers are only the wealthiest, most sophisticated sort of people—the kind of people who buy expensive cars, perfumes and jewelry.

INDONESIAN LITERATURE: JOURNALISTS, POETS AND REVOLUTIONARIES

Ask a foreigner to name a famous Indonesian writer, and you'll almost certainly get a blank look. To be honest, even if you ask an Indonesian to name a famous Indonesian writer you might get a blank look. But Indonesia actually has an exciting literary culture—full of romantically doomed poets from times past, fiercely outspoken female litterateurs from times present, and out-there innovators setting the tone for times to come.

Right Controversial Sastra Wangi author Ayu Utami.

Indonesia's modern literary culture is a young one, little more than a century old. The first proper Indonesian-language novel, Merari Siregar's *Azab dan Sengsara*, only appeared in 1920. Despite what you'll often be told, this isn't really because Indonesia is primarily a land of oral storytelling (there are few countries on earth where popular storytelling wasn't primarily oral until a couple of centuries ago). It's because Bahasa Indonesia only became a language of mass literacy from the turn of the 20th century. Before that there was an ancient writing culture in the form of *hikayat* and *babad*—chronicles penned in the numerous regional languages, especially Javanese.

But once Indonesian took off as a written national language, a new literary canon quickly came into being. Early

The Lontar Foundation

For a long time finding Indonesian literature in English translation was tough. But these days there's a whole lot of it, thanks to the work of a brilliant not-for-profit organization based in Jakarta. The Lontar Foundation puts out an ever-growing list of translations of Indonesian novels and story collections—from 1920s classics to cutting-edge modern works. You'll find their distinctively designed books, with sleek black spines and contemporary art of the covers, in English-language bookshops all over Indonesia.

journalists started Indonesia's strong tradition of the *cerpen*—*cerita pendek*, or "short story". Many Indonesian

Pramoedya Anata Toer

newspapers still keep this tradition alive, publishing short fiction in their Sunday editions. Poets followed, and then novelists, with the first rush of books appearing in the 1920s. Look out for Marah Roesli's *Sitti Nurbaya* and Abdoel Moeis' *Salah Asuhan* (published as *Never the Twain* in English) from this period. The so-called "1945 Generation" drove Indo-Lit forward against the fiery backdrop of revolution: Idrus with his starkly chiseled prose, a sort of Indonesian answer to Hemingway; and Chairul Anwar, a rebel poet of positively Byronic character who died young (of either TB or syphilis, depending who you ask). And then, in the post-war years, the big beasts emerged, and none bigger than Pramoedya Anata Toer...

IS PRAMOEDYA ANY GOOD?

Pramoedya routinely tops lists of "books about Indonesia" compiled by Western journalists who've never read a word Pramoedya wrote. He's simply the only Indonesian author people have ever heard of. I'll just come out and say it now: I've never been keen on Pram's books. I *should* like them: they take early 20th-century Indonesian history as their backdrop, and that's a period I find fascinating. But his celebrated *Buru Quartet*, a four-book saga centering on a young journalist named Minke in the years of the first stirring of Indonesian nationalism, are pretty heavy going. Some of his other books, such as *The Girl from the Coast* (*Gadis Pantai*), are much more readable, and Pramoedya's

life story is astonishing—he was one of the few people to have been imprisoned for his politics by the Dutch, by Sukarno's government, and by the Suharto regime alike, and the Buru Quartet was partially penned during his long internment in the 1970s. But if you're looking for an introduction to "classic" Indonesian literature, I'd sooner suggest you check out Pram's contemporary, Mochtar Lubis. His unsettling novella *Tiger!* (*Harimau!*) is brilliant.

CONTEMPORARY INDO-LIT

Since the 1990s high-level Indonesian literature has often thrown up edgy and exciting voices. The first serious movers and shakers were women writers whose work was known collectively as the

Sastra Wangi. This means "Fragrant Literature", but there wasn't much that was delicate or flowery about the voices of Ayu Utami and Djenar Maesa Ayu—seriously forthright authors happy to write about sex without any coyness. It's a shame their work isn't more easily available in English, but look out for Ayu Utami's brilliant *Saman*, and Djenar Maesa Ayu's *They Say I'm a Monkey*. Elsewhere, at the somewhat less "literary" end of the Indonesian book market, Andrea Hirata scored a hit with his *Laskar Pelangi* in 2005 (later translated as *The Rainbow Troops*). It's the sort of story usually described as "heartwarming", a tale of poor kids overcoming adversity.

Meanwhile, at the cutting edge of Indonesian literature, authors like Gus tf Sakai and Eka Kurniawan have been ditching the realism of Pramoedya and Mochtar Lubis to come up with something much more radical—a sort of Indonesian magical-realism. Kurniawan's debut in English translation, the wildly wacky *Beauty is a Wound*, got critics in London and New York in a tizzy, and he's become something of an international literary celebrity along the lines of Marquez and Murakami. Elsewhere, Leila S. Chudori also won critical acclaim for her epic saga of Indonesia's dark past, *Pulang* (published as *Home* in English).

Of course, you only need to go into a big Indonesian bookshop (Gramedia is the major chain) to see that none of this literary stuff has much relevance for most of the book-buying public. What you'll find on the shelves are dozens of pulpy romances, teen horror stories, depressingly predictable conspiracy theory polemics, self-help books—oh, and translations of Eriko Ono's *Miiko* stories, a Japanese manga series for children, sold in Gramedia in vast quantities to twenty-something professionals!

Books on Indonesia by **Bules**

There are some very good books about Indonesia by foreigners—and some very bad ones too, but I won't mention them here! Instead here are three of my favorite Indonesia travel books from the last few years.

Indonesia, Etc. by Elizabeth Pisani—This is the sort of travel book lovers of Indonesia were waiting for: an intrepid journey taking in distant points of the archipelago, by an author who knows the country extremely well.

After the Ancestors by Andrew Beatty—I loved Beatty's previous book, *A Shadow Falls*, an anthropologist's account of village life in Java. But this more recent title totally bowled me over—a nonfiction narrative from the remote island of Nias with positively Shakespearean qualities.

Crazy Little Heaven by Mark Heyward—There's a lovely, affectionate tone to this book, which combines the tale of an epic trek through Kalimantan with a memoir of two decades living in Indonesia.

CHAPTER 5

INDONESIANS AT PLAY

Whether it's stirring up a storm on the terraces at a soccer match, or stepping into the wild on a volcano-climbing adventure, Indonesians have all sorts of ways to play. And out on the road the younger generations are forging a new travel style, with a blogosphere-driven backpacking revolution taking hip young adventurers from Jakarta and Surabaya to the far reaches of the archipelago—where they might just dabble in a little surfing and diving. They'll still have to remember to bring back some *oleh-oleh* for the folks at home, though…

HEADING FOR THE HILLS: INDONESIANS ON HOLIDAY

Every weekend of the year, from one end of the country to the other, a limitless legion of SUVs comes cascading out of the big cities, bound for the nearest bit of elevated altitude; families swamp the airports as they queue for budget airline flights; and convoys of air-con coaches rumble out onto the highways, bearing armies of suburban housewives in the direction of *obyek wisata* ("tourism objects"—as likely to be a shabby theme park as a historical attraction) and oleh-oleh-buying opportunities.

Never miss a photo op! Indonesian tourists at Tanah Lot in Bali.

The Indonesian Tourism Ministry estimates that Indonesian domestic tourists take around 250 million trips annually. Statistically, that equates to pretty much one domestic holiday a year for every Indonesian, but given that many millions of Indonesians from the lower rungs of the economic ladder take no holidays at all, it really represents a whole bunch of wealthier people taking a whole bunch of trips. Make no mistake, when it comes to travel, Indonesia is a nation on the move.

WEEKENDS AWAY

I'm pretty sure you'd be able to see it from outer space: a vast tide of cars and buses creeping from Jakarta towards Puncak, and from Surabaya towards Batu-Malang, on any given Saturday. A middle-class weekend exodus to the mountains is an Indonesian tradition that dates back to the colonial era, when overheated Dutch families would head for misty hill stations, where it was cool enough to call for a blanket at night, and where such wildly exotic foodstuffs as apples and potatoes grow. These places were Indonesia's first resorts, and they're still where millions of city-dwellers travel each weekend, in the name of "refreshing" (the Indonesian word is *menyegar-*

kan, but people tend to use the English term when talking about travel).

Inevitably, visions of misty mountain tranquility are a thing of the past in most hill stations these days. Instead you get sprawling conurbations of villas with a few hints of karaoke parlor sleaze on the peripheries. And traffic—the most insane traffic imaginable. Personally, I struggle to find any "refreshing" qualities in a hill resort on a weekend. But on a quiet weekday there is a certain melancholy charm, especially in the smaller places that serve the smaller cities; a sort of kitschy nostalgia, akin to that of old-time seaside resorts in Britain and the East Coast USA.

INDONESIAN HILL RESORTS: Some Cool Locations (Once You Get There)

BATU The East Java town of Batu (often called "Batu-Malang") is the classic Indonesian hill resort. Set in a bowl of high green mountains, it was originally a genteel getaway for colonial folks. These days it's a brash, noisy carnival of a place, and half the population of Surabaya seems to decamp there every Saturday.

PUNCAK The classic mountain destination for the Jakarta residents is the Puncak area. On a weekday the snaking road that winds up through the tea gardens to this 4,750-foot (1,448-meter) pass is a delightful drive; on the weekends it's a vision of gridlocked hell!

BERASTAGI The gritty North Sumatra megalopolis of Medan is just far enough away to save Berastagi from being utterly overwhelmed each weekend, and there are some great volcano-climbing opportunities in the vicinity.

BERASTAGI

PUNCAK

BATU

VACATION TIME

Indonesian domestic tourism still tends to be dominated by pretty conventional middle class family holidays in pretty conventional destinations. In the word association game, "holiday" in Indonesia generally prompts immediate thoughts of "Bali". Annual domestic tourist figures for Bali are almost double those for international visitors, and most of those domestic tourists head for midrange resorts in the island's insanely crowded south. Yogyakarta is the other major destination, where domestic tourists massively outnumber foreigners. Traditional Indonesian holidays to these places tend to feature a lot of time in the hotel; a lot of eating; and a lot of souvenir-buying. And if the holiday budget stretches to an overseas trip, chances are it'll feature more of the same in either Singapore or Hong Kong. The important thing is that you go with family and friends; that you spend big; and that you come home soon—which is why, for so many Indonesians, the foreign backpackers who pass through their country with tight budgets and extended timescales, and sometimes even without any companions, are so utterly inexplicable.

Left Student hiking clubs leave their mark in Dieng.

Above Striking a pose in upland Java—a selfie stick is a modern Indonesian travel essential.

Things are changing, however, when it comes to Indonesian attitudes to travel. In the last decade a social media-driven domestic backpacking culture and a craze for adventure travel have gone big, and at the sophisticated, luxury end of the travel market too, domestic tourists have started to think outside of the Bali box. But you still won't find many Indonesians going traveling on their own—that would just be too weird!

Where's my oleh-oleh?

Whether it's a day trip to a local hill resort, or a trip of a lifetime to the capitals of Europe, there is one essential feature of any Indonesian holiday: the buying of oleh-oleh, souvenir gifts for friends and family back home. In fact, it sometimes seems that the only reason to go on holiday is to bring back vast volumes of tacky tee shirts, "I heart Bali" keyrings and fridge magnets, and local "specialty" snacks. Go to the hangar-like oleh-oleh emporiums of Yogyakarta and Bali, and you'll see holidaying housewives literally filling shopping carts to the brim with this stuff. So if you want to do right by your Indonesian friends, don't forget to bring back oleh-oleh for them when you take a trip.

BEDUGUL Domestic tourists and Denpasar residents have traditionally left Ubud to the eating, praying, loving foreigners, and headed higher into Bali's mountains, especially to the volcanic crater of Bedugul. This is one hill resort that's clung onto some of its old-time charm, with a picture-perfect lake and a lovely botanical garden.

TAWANGMANGU This is one of the second-string hill resorts that I always enjoy visiting during my journeys around Java. Sitting high on the slopes of Gunung Lawu, it's a bit ramshackle, and it's pretty much a ghost town of a weekday—but you can get a very tasty plate of rabbit sate from the roadside stalls.

BEDUGUL

TAWANGMANGU

Indonesia's Travel Blog Scene:
An Interview with Vira and Mumum of Indohoy

There are thousands of Indonesian backpackers hitting the road these days, and travel bloggers seem to have had a key role to play in this coolest of trends. The first to gain widespread attention was Trinity, whose Indonesian-language Naked Traveler blog has been turned into a series of bestselling books (the "naked" of the title is a clever inter-lingual pun on the Indonesian word *nekat*, which means something along the lines of "reckless"). But my favorite Indonesian travel bloggers have always been Mumun and Vira, the women behind the totally awesome Indohoy.com. Helpfully for foreigners, they blog in English. They get to some properly off-the-beaten track places, as well as taking original approaches to mainstream destinations. They're also a whole lot of fun. I caught up with them to get their insider views on Indonesia's travel scene.

Indohoy Mumun (left) and Vira (right).

Ok, first up, please introduce yourselves: who are you, where are you from, what are your day jobs? (Actually, do you guys still have day jobs? You seem to be traveling the whole time these days...)

Vira: I'm Vira Zoelfikar from Indonesia, I've been a Jakarta resident for almost 14 years. I'm a freelance writer for a local TV station—that allows me to travel anytime as long as I get an Internet connection.

Mumun: I'm Murni Ridha, known to my friends as Mumun. Born and raised in Bandung, but of pure Bugis blood. Who I am is a big question. I currently work at Wego, a metasearch for travel. But seriously, we're not always on the road.

Why did Indonesia suddenly get the backpacking bug—and why did it take so long for Indonesians to start truly embracing travel in their own country?

Vira: I think the budget airlines started the travel boom in Indonesia, especially AirAsia. Indonesia is huge, and traveling by plane really helps us get around. Plus, more people are connected online so we're more aware about traveling

chances we could have, and the awesome places in the country that we didn't know about. I also think Trinity Traveler helped spreading the travel virus through her bestselling *Naked Traveler* books.

Why did you decide to write in English when you first started Indohoy?

Vira: Our intention was (and still is) to give information about traveling in Indonesia to foreigners because we found zero websites on that topic at the time, and we thought it could help Indonesian tourism. Plus, Mumun thinks in English anyway, so I don't see her ever blogging in Indonesian.

Mumun: Vira knows me well, I don't do well in Indonesian. There's still not many sites that are consistent or equipped with practical information, so I think we've secured our place pretty well. Honestly, Indonesia could do with a few more.

Indohoy—great name! Which one of you came up with it? ("Indohoy" is a pun on the old-fashioned Indonesian euphemism "*in da hoy*" which comes from the Dutch, and means, well, "a roll in the hay"...)

Vira: Thanks. Actually neither of us came up with the name. There were seven of us starting the website and one of the other guys came up with the name, but I forgot whom. The other five backed out even before Indohoy was launched online.

Left Bali is the ultimate travel destination for Indonesians. It sees more than twice as many domestic tourists as foreigners each year.

Mumun: I'm glad you get it. The next generation has no idea how funny it is!

There seems to be a real sense of community amongst travel bloggers in Indonesia. Why do you think that is?

Mumun: We're very social. Individualism isn't something common in our society, even in the cities. Most Indonesians still think it's weird to do things alone, like going to the movies or having a meal at a restaurant. So, it's always about a bunch of people and encouraging each other. And it's not just the travel blogger community. EVERYTHING has a community in Indonesia.

As with most of the Indonesian blogosphere, girls seem to rule in the travel blogging scene. Are the boys all at home playing PlayStation, or what?

Vira: I've asked the same question and unfortunately I can only come up with my own assumption: boys are too lazy to write and remember the details of their adventures. Case in point: my husband Diyan. He'd rather read comics or 9gag when I'm busy with my blog.

Successful travel bloggers often start to get commercial opportunities. How do you keep it "real", and keep your passion as it starts to turn from a hobby into work?

Vira: Actually, we've been keeping it real by not making a living out of our blog. However, we do take a few sponsorships, paid endorsements and product placements, and we're committed to always disclosing it to our readers. Also, I've gone back to my old hobby, drawing, and Mumun to hers, analyzing pop music. So I guess the key is to always have something as a pure hobby, and not selling out (too much).

Mumun: Vira pretty much says it all. What's real is that if you make your hobby into a living, "real" becomes the need to support yourself.

Name one thing you love about travel in Indonesia and one thing you don't like about travel in Indonesia...

Vira: I love that there are still so many "hidden" places. I don't like the humidity.

Mumun: I both love and hate the uncertainty, whether being information availability, transportation schedules, or things still being very raw. Does that make sense?

You've been traveling together for years now. Do you ever fight when you're on the road?

Mumun: This is something a lot of people ask us. Is there something

wrong with people traveling together? Is there more hate than love when traveling? Arguments but no fights...

If you could recommend one unusual, overlooked place in Indonesia, where would it be? And is there one place in Indonesia you haven't been to yet that you really want to visit?

Vira: I'd recommend Betung Kerihun National Park in Kalimantan Barat, especially if you're into trekking. I have many places in Indonesia that I want to visit, but if I have to pick one (gosh, you're so mean!) maybe... it would be Bawean Island. Or any white sand beach in Papua. Or the whole Sumba Island. Darn, I haven't even been to Kupang and Rote Island!

Mumun: Recently, I've fallen for Banda Neira. I don't usually travel to the same destination twice in the same year, other than Bali, but Banda Neira was an exception for many reasons. It's just got everything. Sea, sand, mountains, and oh-so-much history. To think these small islands drove the whole world insane in the past just blows my mind. I've learned so much from such a small archipelago and I'd revisit in a blink of an eye if I could afford it. I recommend it! One place I really want to visit: Saumlaki in Tanimbar Island. I've heard of a spectacular diving site and crazy-ass cloth weaving there. I want to see it!

www.indohoy.com

Student backpackers taking in the views over the Dieng Plateau in central Java.

SPORT IN INDONESIA

From dirt patches in little villages in the nether reaches of Nusa Tenggara to floodlit stadiums in the megalopolises of Java, there's a game afoot in Indonesia. Popular sports run a broad gamut from traditional combat rituals to basketball, and Indonesia throws up international success in the lighter weight categories of professional boxing from time to time— Chris "The Dragon" John, who retired in 2013, is an 18-time WBA World Featherweight champion. But there's no mistaking which sport is truly closest to the nation's heart.

Above Field of dreams— Dipta soccer stadium in Bali.

Left Raw talent—most Indonesian kids make first contact with a soccer ball as soon as they can walk.

THE SOCCER ARCHIPELAGO

Wherever I go, from Sumatra to Sulawesi, whenever people learn where I'm from their eyes light up: "From England? Have you met Wayne Rooney, then?" Yes, Indonesia is all about soccer. As someone whose personal sporting tastes incline more to surfing and mountain-climbing, I'm at a distinct social disadvantage in a nation where it's not unusual to run into toothless grandpas who can declaim authoritatively on the politics of the English Premier League. But even I can appreciate the sheer passion for soccer

in Indonesia, where every kampung in the country has its own miniature Messi and pint-sized Ronaldo, triumphing in barefoot pickup games. But the sport where Indonesia actually excels in international competition is not soccer…

BADMINTON BEHEMOTH

The only sport where Indonesia can claim consistent success is played not with a leather ball, but with two lightweight rackets and a shuttlecock. That's right—badminton, of all things, is the only sporting field where Indonesian athletes regularly bring home

Below Any open space offers an opportunity for a casual game!

Above and left Dedication and devotion—fans of Jakarta's Persija soccer team heading to a match by any possible means.

Left Olympic badminton medalist Taufik Hidayat.
Above Doubles champs Hendra Setiawan and Mohammad Ahsan on the attack.

gold. The national team routinely ranks in the world top five—tussling with the likes of China and Japan for supremacy—and Indonesia has won gold medals for badminton in virtually every Olympics in the last fifty years. Soccer aficionados, gloomily regarding their national team's woeful international performances, can only look on with bewildered jealousy.

Just why Indonesia is so good at badminton is hard to work out, but one feature of Indonesian badminton that's often noted by observers is the prominence of ethnic Chinese players. In fact, it's sometimes said that the sport of badminton is Indonesia's ultimate beacon of ethnic inclusivity. You won't often find successful Chinese-Indonesian athletes in other sports—and especially

not in soccer. But even when official discrimination against Indonesians of Chinese origin was at its worst in the 1970s and 1980s, ethnic Chinese badminton stars like Liem Swie King and Hariamanto Kartono were bestriding the globe. The game was probably actually introduced to Indonesia by ethnic Chinese back in the late colonial era, which might be why they stayed so important in the sport, even when the official odds were stacked against them.

As well as its ethnic inclusivity, the success of Indonesian badminton probably has a good deal to do with the fact that the All Indonesian Badminton Association is a well-run, professional organization, with a reputation for organizing effective training programs, unlike—whisper it!—certain other sporting bodies in Indonesia. Mind you, even badminton's not always squeaky clean: two Indonesian players were kicked out of the 2012 London Olympics for match fixing.

Sergio van Dijk

Indonesia's "International" Players

When it comes to bolstering its international side, the Football Association of Indonesia is always happy to broaden its horizons. Dutchmen of Indonesian heritage with serious soccer skills are always a popular choice, so long as they're ready to ditch their Dutch passports (Indonesia doesn't allow dual citizenship). Sergio van Dijk and Irfan Bachdim were both born in the Netherlands. But the most outstanding—in every sense—adopted Indonesian in the national squad of recent years has been one Cristian Gonzáles. Standing a head taller than most of his teammates, Gonzáles was actually originally from Uruguay, and only came to play soccer in Indonesia in 2003 after a lackluster, decade-long career in South America. In 2010 he was granted Indonesian citizenship, just in time to score twice during his international debut against Timor-Leste.

Indonesian Soccer:
An Interview with Antony Sutton

The writer Antony Sutton—another expat Brit in Indonesia—has been documenting the soccer scene here for over a decade through his Jakarta Casual blog, which is a great read even for a non-soccer fan like me. I caught up with him to get his thoughts on the beautiful game...

Antony Sutton with Persebaya fans.

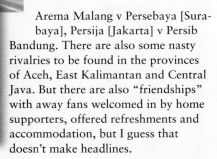

Left Irfan Bachdim
Far left Arema Malang fans.
Bottom left Indonesia vs Laos in a regional international match.

Indonesia has some pretty hardcore fans, and some pretty nasty rivalries. Which teams have the most notorious followers, and which are the most intense rivalries?

Arema Malang v Persebaya [Surabaya], Persija [Jakarta] v Persib Bandung. There are also some nasty rivalries to be found in the provinces of Aceh, East Kalimantan and Central Java. But there are also "friendships" with away fans welcomed in by home supporters, offered refreshments and accommodation, but I guess that doesn't make headlines.

Can you sum up the Indonesian game in a nutshell, and tell us what makes it special?

Indonesian soccer reflects Indonesia. At times beautiful, at times chaotic, filled with WTF moments and never dull. Tourists flock to Bromo, Borobudur, and Bali and quite rightly. But soccer offers an insight to Indonesians at play, and for me there is no finer sight nor sound in Indonesia than a full terrace getting behind their team, be it in Malang, Solo, Bandung, Yogyakarta, Semarang, Jakarta or Surabaya. Indonesian soccer may not have much of an international impact, but fan culture is streets ahead of anywhere else in the region and that is something Indonesians should be proud of.

Like the English Premier League, the Indonesia Super League has its shipped-in foreign players—I used to run into some of them in bars in Surabaya back in the day. Any thoughts on that?

Sometimes the easy answer is to bring in a foreign player, but many of those are not necessarily better than local lads, and if Indonesia is to make its mark regionally it is the local lads who need to make an impact, not an aging thirtysomething who has run out of options elsewhere. That said, some foreign players have had a massive impact and continue to be shunted from club to club, but it comes at a price.

Why doesn't this huge, soccer-mad nation, with plenty of raw talent out in the kampungs, totally dominate the game in Asia? What's holding them back?

Players are badly advised, clubs, such as they are, are poorly run, and as for the PSSI [Football Association of Indonesia], there are some good people there trying to do a job but the circumstances do not allow it.

Clubs like Persib Bandung, and Arema could be massive—and I mean massive—beyond the shores of Indonesia if only the game was marketed and sold properly. But so many of those with responsibility for moving the game forward come from a red tape culture, not an entrepreneurial culture. They see putting up obstacles as a good thing.

The word "potential" is widely used but there is no potential until the mindset changes. Losing 10-0 in a World Cup Qualifier [to Bahrain, of all places, in 2012], or getting suspended by FIFA [in 2015, because of government interference in the management of the national league] would be national disasters in other soccer-mad countries. Not in Indonesia where the red tape merchants use the bad news as a way to support their petty nationalist credentials.

Do you have any tips or pointers for a foreigner looking to get a taste of the Indonesian game?

Read Jakarta Casual and don't book your holiday around the fixture lists! Jam karet extends to the beautiful game!

www.jakartacasual.blogspot.com

Only in Indonesia: Weird and Wonderful Traditional Sports

Modern competitive sports aside, some of Indonesia's regional sporting specialties make for dramatic—and at times downright dangerous—spectacles. There are variations of buffalo and bull racing in lots of places around the country, sometimes in flooded rice fields, sometimes on dry dirt. The animals are always yoked in pairs, with a daredevil jockey riding a wooden sled behind. You'll find races in Sumbawa and western Bali, but the highest-octane bull races take place in Madura in August and September.

There are fighting sports too, where two contestants go head

to head with weapons. In Lombok it's rattan sticks in the sport known as *peresean*, while in around Ruteng in Flores it's vicious whips for the ritual contest called *caci*. But the most spectacular of all contests, with sport and ceremony combining in a heady ferment, is the annual Pasola contest in Sumba, where neighboring communities, mounted on horseback, go to war against one another armed with wooden spears. The spears were only blunted by officialdom within the last generation, and even so bloodshed is common. It beats even the most exciting soccer match any day, if you ask me.

Left Peresean fight in Lombok.
Below The Pasola in Sumba.

Above Madura bull racing.

Pencak Silat

Besides soccer, badminton—and perhaps competitive surfing—Indonesia's only other obvious contender for status of "national sport" is the martial art known as pencak silat. This name is actually a catch-all term for the dozens of traditional fighting styles to be found in Indonesia. Virtually every region and ethnic group has its own martial traditions, and pencak silat features a huge diversity of styles and techniques, both armed and unarmed. However, virtually all these regional varieties have traditionally been seen as more than mere sports or martial skills: at its highest level pencak silat is usually regarded as having a spiritual element, and the greatest masters are often rumored to have skills that stray into the realms of the supernatural.

UNDERWATER INDONESIA: THE ULTIMATE DIVE DESTINATION

There's a lot going on beneath the surface in Indonesia. You only need to look at the map to figure it out: the country takes up by far the single biggest chunk of the so-called "coral triangle", the three-cornered swath of shallow sea stretching from the northernmost tip of the Philippines to the South Pacific where the world's greatest wealth of tropical marine life is to be found. No surprise, then, that this is the best destination for diving and snorkeling on earth.

Diving was the one outdoors sport—besides golf!—that wealthy Indonesians signed up for in significant numbers, even before young suburbanites with disposable incomes started buying backpacks and setting up travel blogs. I once asked a veteran dive school operator why she thought this might be the case, and she reckoned that middle class Indonesians were following the lead of other Asian nations: scuba diving tourists from Japan, Korea, and Singapore have been coming to Indone-

Above Look behind you! A close encounter with a manta ray in Bali.

Clear waters and coral reefs hem many of Indonesia's shores.

Up close and personal with a whale shark in the depths off Papua.

Above Underwater paradise—the coral gardens of Bunaken off the northernmost tip of Sulawesi.
Left Green turtle

sia in significant numbers for decades. She also suggested that the association of diving with expensive equipment and exclusive resorts might be important—ah, our old friend gengsi again! But one thing's for sure: everyone forgets about status once they're under the water and into the blue beyond. Indonesia has warm, clear seas, home to something like 3,000 species of fish, and dive sites ranging from wrecks to huge coral walls.

There is high-quality diving scattered, quite literally, from one end of the country to the other—starting with Pulau Weh off the top end of Sumatra, with more decent diving around Bangka and Belitung, and in the Karimunjawa Islands which drift tantalizingly off the north coast of Java. But the greatest wealth of undersea adventure is to be found in the eastern half of the archipelago. Eastern Bali has some solid—and solidly accessible—dive sites, and plenty of long-established facilities. There's more around the Gili Islands off Lombok too. This is diving for the masses though. The more exclusive action is out amongst the easternmost islands, where there are both isolated resorts and plenty of high-end live-aboard operators: Bunaken at the furthest extremity of Sulawesi; the Togeans; the Komodo National Park; Banda; Wakatobi; Alor. Then there's one of the most fabled diving destinations on earth, Raja Ampat, a mass of more than 1,500 islands, rising like green knuckles from a cobalt sea of the northwestern end of Papua.

Island Snorkeling

If you don't have the cash or the inclination to dive you can still explore Indonesia's undersea worlds. There's reasonable snorkeling right off the beaches in a few places in Bali, including Padangbai and Amed (though I'd say that Bali's best snorkeling is around the offshore islands of Nusa Penida and Nusa Lembongan), and off the Gili Islands too. Karimunjawa also has great snorkeling, and no crowds, while in the other direction there's a little gem of a snorkeling spot called Pantai Merah ("Red Beach") in the Komodo National Park. You can do at least some snorkeling at most of the other diving destinations too, including the legendary Raja Ampat—though you might feel like a bit of a poor relation to the guys and gals with the scuba gear...

A SURFER'S PARADISE: EXPLORING INDONESIA'S TOP SURF SPOTS

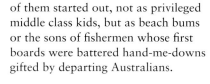

The story of surfing in Indonesia begins, inevitably, in Bali. Way back in the 1930s, the expat American hotelier Bob Koke paddled out on his longboard at Kuta Beach and rode the first Indonesian wave. But it wasn't until the start of the 1970s, that surfing in Indonesia really found its feet. Visiting Australian surfers struck out beyond Kuta's hippie hangout, blazing trails through the scrubby badlands of the Bukit Peninsula to find ethereal reef breaks at the bottom of craggy limestone cliffs—Uluwatu, Padang-Padang, Bingin; places that would become household names in the surfing world in the following decade.

Before long intrepid surf explorers were setting their sights beyond Bali, to Lombok and Sumbawa, the stormy southern littoral of Java, and to Sumatra's necklace of offshore islands. It was surfing that first brought me to Indonesia, and I like to think that I turned up in just in time to catch the tail-end of this great bout of truly intrepid surf travel in the archipelago. At the turn of the 21st century there were still plenty of tousle-headed young men from California, Cornwall, and Cronulla, touching down in Bali then vanishing into the outer reaches of Indonesia with minimal funds, to reappear months later, emaciated, scarred, and stoked, with decent grasp of Bahasa Indonesia and a wild look in their eyes. Even the places that were already firmly on the surf tourism circuit were sometimes still rough and ready prospects at that time. When I first visited Hu'u in Sumbawa, contact with home required an hour-long ride on the back of a motorbike up a potholed road to the one-horse town of Dompu. These days you can probably pick up a Wi-Fi signal in the lineup…

Bali's Padang-Padang beach, location of one of Indonesia's most extreme reef breaks.

LOCAL HEROES

Global surf travel often comes in for criticism, from both environmentalists horrified by inappropriate tourism developments on remote beaches, and from those who detect a hint of neocolonialism in its language of exploration and annexation. There's something to be said for all that, but the strength of surf tourism in countries like Indonesia is that the local people it affects positively tend to come from marginal communities. There are thousands of fanatical Indonesia surfers today, and a multimillion dollar surf industry to serve them. The country dominates the Asian competitive surfing circuit, and has professional surfers of global stature. And most of them started out, not as privileged middle class kids, but as beach bums or the sons of fishermen whose first boards were battered hand-me-downs gifted by departing Australians.

Above and left Where it all began—Uluwatu, Bali's original surf hotspot.

Going big in Bali

From T-land to G-land: Indonesia's Surf Geography

Indonesia's waves are generated in the deep storm systems of the Indian Ocean, and its best surf is to be found on the country's southern and western coastal arc. The best season for surfing is the dry season, from late April to early October. During the wet months the storm systems track further south and the winds blow onshore—though Bali still delivers the goods at this time on its alternate, east-facing coast.

There are waves all the way down the west coast of the Sumatran mainland, including at the laidback surf camp scene at Krui in Lampung province. But the serious Sumatran surf is offshore, in the string of islands that trace the coast, from Nias through the Mentawai Islands to Enggano. This was once true frontier territory, though these days it's the province of the luxury surf charter boat. Java's southern coast is wild and wave-lashed, and though much of it is made up of black sand beaches that struggle to handle the driving Indian Ocean swells, there are legendary waves here and there—not least One-Palm Point on Panaitan Island in the west, and G-Land in the east—plus tamer spots like Batu Karas and Pacitan. Then there's Bali, which needs little introduction, followed by Lombok with its well-established local surf scene, through wilder shores in Sumbawa and Sumba, all the way to Nembrala on the little island of Rote off Timor, home to the T-Land break.

That's not the end of it, though. Indonesia has another coastline, facing another massive, swell-generating body of water—you'll find waves on the northern shores of Papua and the outer limits of Maluku too.

A lucky traveler slots into a backhand barrel, somewhere in the Mentawai Islands.

Finding Your Feet: Beginner Surf Spots

Most of Indonesia's surf is over coral or limestone reefs, and most of the waves are seriously challenging. But there are a few options if you're a total beginner. The single best place to start from scratch is where it all began, Kuta Beach in Bali. It's that rare thing in Indonesia—a relatively easy-going beach break. And it has loads of surf schools, freelance instructors, and board hire places. Beyond Kuta there really aren't too many places suited to starting out, but Batu Karas in Java, on the coast west of Cilacap, is one good option—a laidback little surf community with friendly wet season waves.

The first generation of Indonesian pro surfers came, unsurprisingly, from Bali—legendary figures including Made Switra (now a soul-surfing artist) and Rizal Tanjung (who still ranks as Indonesian surf royalty, and owns a couple of surf shops and a clothing brand).

Current superstar, Raditya Rondi, whose name is mentioned in the same breath as the very greatest Australian and Hawaiian surfers, is also from Bali. But these days elite athletes often emerge from little fishing villages all across Indonesia—guys like Dede Suryana from Cimaja in West Java. And then there's a certain hotshot from Sumbawa…

When my surfing buddy Russ and I first went to Hu'u in Sumbawa, home of the legendary Lakey Peak break, we met a local nine-year-old called Oney. We taught him card games, and he took us to meet his dad, who lived in a wooden hut in the forest behind the isolated Cobblestones break. Oney had a knack for backchat in idiosyncratic surfer-taught English, and even riding a massively oversized secondhand board, you could see that he had talent. Many years later, I happened to be flicking through an Australian surf mag when I happened upon a double-page spread featuring one Oney Anwar—by that time a Rip Curl-sponsored professional, living and competing in Australia. Surfing had taken him a very long way from a remote village in one of the poorest parts of Indonesia.

INTO THE WILD:
INDONESIA'S GREAT OUTDOORS

Indonesia might be the fourth most populous country on the planet, but it is still home to vast wild spaces. A glance of a satellite image of the archipelago throws it all into stark relief. Despite the destructive advances of plantation agriculture, great swaths of Sumatra, Borneo, and Papua are still blanketed with jungle, and even ultra-crowded Java has sizable pockets of forested wilderness. And then there are the mountains: Indonesia's volcanic geology has provided it with legions of spectacular peaks.

Below The wilderness isn't always a place of solitude! Popular spots like Dieng can be packed with student hikers during holiday weekends.

Bottom Hikers on the trail around the mighty Rinjani caldera on Lombok.

Traditional Indonesian attitudes towards the country's wildernesses have been laced with suspicion. Forests and mountains were the haunt of outlaws, dangerous animals—and ghosts. Anyone who actually wanted to go to such places was probably some kind of deviant. But things have changed. There has always been a minority of outdoors enthusiasts—mainly made up of university mountaineering clubs. But their ranks have swelled massively since middle class Indonesia caught the travel bug. Boutiques selling hiking and camping gear have sprouted in towns across the country, and the most popular mountains of Java and Sumatra are besieged by gangs of young climbers every weekend. Elsewhere, jungle trekking, whitewater rafting, canyoning and mountain-biking have all boomed too.

MOUNTAINEERING, INDONESIAN STYLE

Volcanoes are not like other mountains. Generally there's no gentle lead-up through rolling foothills, and no meandering, modulated ascent across varying contours. Volcanoes tend to rear monstrously from near-sea level, and rocket up towards the 10,000-foot (3,000-meter) mark at an unvarying 45-degree angle. Climbing them is often a relentlessly brutal slog, starting in humid jungle, and ending in searing cold and gale-force winds. But as far as I'm concerned it's all worth it. The

chance to stand two miles (three kilometers) high in a chilly dawn, perched on the brink of a smoking crater and with the whole world laid out at your feet, is one of Indonesia's greatest attractions—even if these days you'll often find yourself sharing the experience with a hundred students, all frantically snapping selfies in the sunrise.

Because of their abrupt profiles, many Indonesian mountains—even those that stretch towards 12,000 feet (3,700 meters)—can be climbed in a single hard hit. The traditional approach is to climb through the night, starting anywhere between dusk and 2 am, depending on the height of the mountain and the altitude of the trailhead. Indonesian student mountaineers tend to head for the hills equipped with massively overladen backpacks, whole cartons of cigarettes, and enough instant noodles and rice to survive on for a month, and then to make their way upwards with endless breaks to smoke, eat, and play cards along the way. They're always great company, but I generally prefer to move a bit faster!

Few of the regularly climbed volcanoes are technically tricky to ascend, and I often run into local kids, 10,000 feet up, in nothing but rubber sandals. But the rapid gains in altitude, and the rapid drops in temperature, mean that climbing Indonesian peaks is never to be taken lightly. People die on the mountains every year, most of them, sad to say, ill-prepared and inexperienced student hikers—the kind who climb in rubber sandals, perhaps. As for where to find prime hiking potential, there are mountains in every province of the country, but most of the dramatic volcanoes are in the southern island arc, from Sumatra to Flores. Java has the highest concentration of dramatic summits, many of them just a short way from the world of offices and campuses in the country's biggest cities.

Gunung Bagging

There was no single organized resource for would-be volcano climbers in Indonesia until a chance meeting between two expat trekkers, Dan Quinn and Andy Dean, high on the slopes of Gunung Lawu in Central Java in 2009. The pair quickly came up with the idea of a "Gunung Bagging" website (*gunung* means "mountain" in Indonesian), and the concept of a definitive list of "Ribus", mountains with all-round elevation drops of at least 1,000 meters (3,300 feet).

"One of the most fascinating things about the list of Ribus is that some of them are so obscure that they have perhaps never been climbed and do not even have recognized names!" says Dan Quinn, who's originally from England.

The Gunung Bagging website quickly became a major hit with both foreigners and local hikers, and the concept of "bagging"—ticking off as many mountains on the list as possible—took hold. A total of 226 mountains across the country have so far been identified as Ribus, with a further 93 that slip in under the "Spesial" category because of their popularity, their challenging nature, or their unusual character. And the Gunung Bagging website has become an unrivalled resource, packed with route reports for mountains across the country, and becoming ever more comprehensive as Indonesia's growing band of gunung baggers add new information to the knowledge bank.
www.gunungbagging.com

Mighty Mountains

RINJANI, LOMBOK 12,224 ft (3,726m) Rinjani was the first major Indonesian mountain I ever climbed, and it's still one of my all-time favorites. It's more of a massif than a single peak, with a vast flooded caldera, and a final summit ascent over scree that's one of the toughest I've encountered. The views from the top are staggering, stretching all the way from Bali to Sumbawa.

PENANGGUNGAN, EAST JAVA 5,423 ft (1,653m) When I lived in Surabaya this little gem of a peak was always my fallback for a quick bit of weekend wilderness time. There are some enigmatic temples to explore on the lower slopes.

DEMPO, SOUTH SUMATRA 10,410 ft (3,173m) If you're looking for a seriously off-the-beaten track volcano to tackle, this Sumatran giant is a brilliant choice—just watch out for the ghost-tigers said to haunt the slopes!

LAWU, EAST JAVA 10,712 ft (3,265m) Straddling the border between East and Central Java, this is one of my very favorite Indonesian hikes. And thanks to the mountain's spiritual significance, sunrise on the summit here has an almost mystical atmosphere.

CHAPTER 6

TRADITIONAL INDONESIA

If all the talk of bloggers, rockers, and celebrities has left you wondering if a "traditional Indonesia" still exists, fear not. Beyond the malls and the multiplexes there's another world, a place of volcanoes and villages, ancient art forms, and spooky stories, where the traces of a turbulent history, packed with princes and pirates, still show through the surface. Let's turn off our smartphones and shut down our social media accounts for a while, and explore the other, older side of Indonesia.

THE RING OF FIRE: IN THE IMPACT ZONE

Stay in Indonesia long enough, and the earth will move for you—and for everyone else too. This is the most geologically volatile nation on the planet, a place where you can never quite rely on the ground beneath your feet.

Indonesia's story begins with an almighty impact. Some 70 million years ago, the Indo-Australian tectonic plate, pivoting northeastwards on the hidden convection currents of the earth's mantle, smacked headlong into the Sunda Plate. The Indo-Australian section drove down underneath the Sunda Plate, creating a deep trench. And as its leading edge melted in the heat below, a mass of volcanoes burst like acne onto the face of the Sunda Plate above. Those volcanoes created the spine of Indonesia as it exists today, and they're still smoking away as the collision continues. The plates are still going head to head, and the subduction zone, tracing the southern coastlines of Indonesia around 200 miles (320 kilometers) offshore, still creaks and crackles with infinite tectonic energy.

Above Fire and brimstone: several active volcanoes produce rich sulfur deposits, which are mined by hardy locals.

Close encounters with active volcanoes—such as Merapi **(above)** and Ijen **(right)**—are a regular feature of hiking in Indonesia.

VOLCANO NATION

Indonesia has more active volcanoes that any other country on earth. They form a long chain from the top of Sumatra, down through Java and Bali, and onwards towards Timor, with others scattered through the less orderly mass of islands further north. There are well over 100 volcanoes considered potentially active nationwide, including 76 that have blown their tops since historical records begun. Volcanic nutrients give Java and Bali the most fertile soils on earth, and the volcanic mountain systems gather and store the moisture that waters the fields. But they also cause trouble.

Many of the active peaks are in a constant state of low-level fury—Kawah Ijen, Gunung Bromo, and Tangkuban Perahu in Java, and Batur in Bali, are all places where you can easily get up close and personal with a smoking crater. And at any given time there is usually at least one volcano having a proper hissy fit somewhere in the country. It's not unusual for volcanic ash clouds to play havoc with Indonesia's airline schedules.

I've peered into plenty of active volcanoes during my travels in Indonesia, but my closest brush with a serious eruption came when I was living in the Central Java city of Yogyakarta back in 2010. Fifteen miles (24 kilometers) north of town stands one of the most famously bad-tempered volcanoes in all of Indonesia, the mighty, 9,610-foot (2,929-meter) Gunung Merapi (the name simply means "Fire Mountain"). It has erupted dozens of times over the past few centuries, but the 2010 bout was a particularly big one. From late September to early November it spat rock and ash in all directions, dev-

Snow in Java? Volcanic ash leaves a ghostly white coating over Yogyakarta after an eruption of nearby Gunung Merapi.

The Biggest Bangs of All

Indonesia's most notorious volcanic eruption of all time took place on the morning of 27 August 1883, when the island of Krakatau in the strait between Java and Sumatra blew its top. It devastated the surrounding coastlines, killed an estimated 36,000 people, and sent some 4.3 cubic miles (18 cubic kilometers) of detritus up into the sky. Meanwhile, a journalist on *The Times* of London made a spelling mistake while writing up a news report of the disaster, ensuring that the volcano responsible would always be better known as "Krakatoa"...

Krakatau, however, was the merest molehill compared to a much bigger bang, 900 miles (1,400 kilometers) east and 68 years earlier. The island of Sumbawa is still dominated by Gunung Tambora today, but this vast volcano is now 4,500 feet (1,400 meters) shorter than it was on the morning of 10 April 1815. That was the day the mountain began to burst apart in the single biggest volcanic explosion in recorded history. Around 100,000 people died; global weather systems went haywire; and a staggering 36 cubic miles (150 cubic kilometers) of ash and dust was fired into the stratosphere.

Mind you, even Tambora pales into insignificance alongside the biggest bang of all. Some 74,000 years ago, the Toba volcano in northern Sumatra erupted. Geologists estimate that it might have expelled twenty times as much debris as Tambora, creating the huge Toba caldera lake in the process.

A vintage image of the deadly 1883 Krakatau eruption.

astating the villages on its lower slopes. By the time it was done it had killed 324 people. Down the road in Yogyakarta the city slowly emptied of students and tourists, and fine volcanic ash settled over everything like pale gray snow.

ON UNSOLID GROUND

At least you can see the volcanoes. And they usually give some warning when they're warming up for one of their periodic displays of pyrotechnics. What really gives Indonesia its atmosphere of tectonic tension is the idea that, at any moment, a pulse of devastating energy could come shooting through the very bedrock.

The pent-up tension along the offshore subduction zone—and along the various other faults and fractures that run through the northern parts of Indonesia—gives rise to endless earthquakes. Most are nothing more than tremors.

But every so often there's a bigger jolt, of the sort to crack roads and topple buildings. Fortunately, most of Indonesia's biggest cities lie away from the Indian Ocean, and so are relatively secure from major quakes. But places like Padang and Yogyakarta have been hit time and again over the centuries.

Nothing quite prepares you for the sensation of an earthquake. Fortunately I've only experienced a few minor tremors. But the memory of waking in a guesthouse in the little Sumatran town of Pagaralam to find my bed, and the whole room, gently rocking back and forth as though someone was trying to lift it free from the earth is something I'll remember forever…

The terrible aftermath of an earthquake in western Sumatra—one of the most quake-prone regions of the country.

Tsunami!

Alongside volcanoes and earthquakes there's a third, terrifying phenomenon to make up Indonesia's tectonic trio: tsunamis. Much of the damage done by Krakatau in 1883 was down to the subsequent tsunamis that swept the Sunda Strait. But the most devastating of all tsunamis was a much more recent event. On 26 December 2004 a huge earthquake west of northern Sumatra thrust up a massive mountain of seawater, which swept across the Indian Ocean. International media gave much attention to the destruction in Thailand, where thousands of foreign tourists were caught up in the carnage, but the worst damage was done in the Indonesian province of Aceh, where hundreds of coastal communities were obliterated, and well over 100,000 people were killed.

TRADERS, RAIDERS AND INTRUDERS: A BRIEF HISTORY OF INDONESIA

Thousand-year-old statuary at Prambanan.

Indonesian history is an epic saga of rebel princes, swaggering traders, and revolutionaries. It comes speckled with spice and fired through with bloody violence. And if it has a single identifiable theme, it's that of myriad foreign influences being injected into the archipelago, and then modified into something uniquely Indonesian. Cramming the whole story into a single book would be a daunting enough task; trying to squeeze it into a few hundred words is flat-out impossible, but we'll take a brisk trot through the basics here!

The first hunter-gatherers turned up in Indonesia around 40,000 years ago, eventually settling into small communities and establishing a clan-based, ancestor-venerating culture—a culture of which you'll still find traces here and there in remote eastern regions of Indonesia today. Indonesian history proper starts much later, however— around 2,000 years ago, as the cultural influence of India began to make itself felt in Java, Borneo, and Sumatra.

Indonesia has always lain at one of the world's great shipping junctions, the midway point between India and China. In the early years of the Current Era Hindu and Buddhist cultural and religious traditions were taken on by indigenous chieftains, given a distinctly local spin, and turned into the beginnings of an "Indonesian" culture. By the dawn of the second millennium CE, western Indonesia was a patchwork of Hindu-Buddhist kingdoms, with a multitude of smaller fiefdoms, less obviously influenced by India, further east.

But by this time new gangs of vagabonding foreigners from the west were heading for Indonesia. First came the Muslims—some from Arabia, but many more from India, Persia, and even

History Off the Beaten Track

The world famous temples at Borobudur and Prambanan are essential sights on any trip to Central Java, but shuffling around amidst the hordes of domestic and international tourists, and dodging the souvenir hawkers, you won't feel very intrepid. But you don't have to go very far to find far more atmospheric temple ruins,

Buddhist temple ruins at Muara Jambi.

places that rarely see a casual visitor, and where you can happily pretend to be Indiana Jones or Lara Croft.

Within a few miles of Prambanan itself, scattered through the range of forested hills to the south, you'll find some beautiful and little known temples: Candi Banyunibo, Candi Ijo, and several others. And there are dozens more temples, all over Java. The area around Malang in East Java is a particularly good place for off-the-beaten-track temple hunting.

But if you really want to feel like an intrepid explorer-archeologist, you'll need to pack your bullwhip and fedora and wing your way to Jambi in Sumatra. This is a remote corner of a vast island, a region of swamps, forests, and lost horizons, and on the banks of the Batang Hari River you'll find a vast complex of red-brick temples, dating from sometime around the 12th century. A few have been tidied up, but there are miles of forest trails, leading to rough ruins, still buried under centuries of leaf mold. You probably won't run into any other travelers here, but there's always the slim chance of encountering a tiger...

Left Dutch officials get a grandstand view of a tiger fight at a Javanese court. These fights were the standard entertainment laid on for European visitors to the royal courts of Java. The Buffalo usually won the battle.

China. After several centuries of contact in the Indonesian ports, their new religion slowly took over in the western parts of the archipelago, just as Hinduism and Buddhism had done before it. At this point, other exotic ships started showing up in the warm Indonesian waters, ships crewed by men with hipster beards, silly hats, and Portuguese accents—the Europeans had arrived.

The Portuguese had sailed halfway around the world in search of nutmeg and cloves. This might seem a bit over-the-top today, but in the 16th century these spices were no mere condiments: they were treasures, worth their weight in gold, and Indonesia was the only place on earth where they grew. The Dutch and the British came trailing after the Portuguese, making their own first Indonesian contacts at the turn of

the 17th century. What followed was a bloody and bad-tempered tussle for power. When the Dutch, Portuguese, and British weren't buying spices, getting drunk, or leering at Indonesian women, they were killing each other or massacring the locals. They were, in short, a bunch of pirates. But they were also the forerunners of the empire, and it was the Dutch who ultimately came out on top in the form of the *Vereenigde Oost-Indische Compagnie*, the Dutch East India Company or VOC.

By the start of the 19th century the old piratical days of spice trading had given way to a more conventional and organized empire, and Indonesia had become the Dutch East Indies—though it wasn't until the start of the 20th century that the very last local kings to hold out against colonial rule were roughly

shaken from their thrones. The empire was ruled by a small cabal of Dutchmen, administered in significant part by coopted local regents, and run as a powerhouse of cash-crop agriculture, providing around a third of all the Netherlands' state revenues. Naturally, there were many Indonesians who thought this was all a bit unfair, and a movement for independence got underway in the early decades of the 20th century. But the Dutch were in no mood to let go of their vast tropical cash cow, and they stifled the movement as best they could. They were in for a nasty shock, however, when World War II began.

WAR AND INDEPENDENCE

In early 1942 the Japanese army swept into Indonesia, ending some three centuries of Dutch rule in one fell swoop. Virtually all of the former imperial masters ended up in gruesome prison camps. Local Indonesians weren't locked up, but they had a rough time under authoritarian Japanese rule. But Indonesian politicians had a chance to organize, and when the Japanese realized they were going to end up on the losing side in the war, they allowed

BUNG KARNO: Indonesia's Flamboyant First President

Indonesian history has featured plenty of flamboyant characters, but few could match the speechifying, philandering demagogue who helmed the country in its first years of nationhood. Sukarno—popularly known as Bung Karno, *bung* being a revolutionary honorific meaning "brother"—was born in Surabaya in 1901. He was a serious and original politician, instrumental in forging the blend of secular nationalism and modified socialism that set the tone in the early days of Indonesian independence.

Ladies' man—Sukarno making friends with Marilyn Monroe.

But forget all of that. What really made Sukarno so memorable was his sheer charisma. Quite simply, the guy was cool, a rock star politician before rock stars even existed. He had the gift of the gab in half a dozen languages, and he was a master of verbal pyrotechnics at the podium. Even if you don't speak Indonesian, grainy recordings of Sukarno in speechifying action in front of vast crowds will likely make the hairs stand up on the back of your neck. And in a country with a tendency for political formality, he had a rare knack for forging casually relaxed connections with whoever he met—from haughty sultans to penniless peasants. Unsurprisingly, he was a big hit with the ladies. Rather like Bill Clinton, he had a rumored ability to turn even the hardest-bitten female journalists weak at the knees with a single glance. He had more wives than Henry VIII (nine, approximately!) and more mistresses than anyone could ever count. Suffice to say, none of the Indonesian leaders who have come since have ever really measured up.

Right The burnt-out car of the British commander, Aubertin Mallaby, whose murder in Surabaya in 1945 as Allied troops tried to get a grip on post-WWII chaos precipitated the "Battle of Surabaya", the first major clash of the revolution, and an episode that earned the East Java capital its nickname, "City of Heroes".

Indonesian nationalism to flourish. On 17 August 1945, two days after the Japanese surrendered to the Allies, the Indonesian leaders Sukarno and Mohammad Hatta issued a unilateral declaration of independence. It would take more than four years of bitter fighting against the returning Dutch before that independence was truly realized, but 17 August is the most iconic date in the Indonesian calendar to this day.

During the 1950s Indonesia struggled to find its feet as a functioning state. There were experiments with a very rickety sort of democracy, and with a kind of soft dictatorship, euphemisti-

cally known as "guided democracy". And all the while Indonesia's flamboyant first president, Sukarno, did his best to keep the country's various opposing forces in balance.

By the mid-1960s this balancing act was becoming impossibly precarious; the economy was in tatters; and catastrophe was threatening. It came in October 1965 when a group of left-leaning, Sukarno-supporting junior army officers organized a putsch against the right-leaning military top brass, supposedly to protect the president from a rumored coup. The ultimate upshot was exactly what they

had feared: they failed to take over the country, and the most senior surviving right-wing general, Suharto, took control of the army. Indonesia's huge Communist Party got the blame for the murders, and its members became the target of a massive, military-sponsored pogrom in which hundreds of thousands of people were slaughtered. And Suharto ended up in charge of Indonesia.

Suharto's thoroughly undemocratic New Order regime ruled the roost for more than three decades. On the one hand the smiling dictator oversaw dramatic economic progress and massive jumps in living standards for ordinary Indonesians; but on the other hand he presided over a grotesquely corrupt system of economic cronyism and political oppression that eventually helped bring the country to its knees during the pan-Asian economic crisis of 1997. Riots on the streets of Jakarta ensued, and Suharto was forced from office.

Since the turn of the 21st century, Indonesia has been making progress as a proper democracy. The former Portuguese outpost of East Timor seceded in bitter and bloody circumstances in late 1999, and several other low-level insurgencies still trouble the fringes of the country. Corruption is still a huge issue, and there are plenty of environmental nightmares, inequalities, and ethnic and religious tensions. But the economy has forged forward, and these days Indonesia looks less like a gimcrack postcolonial nation, than an increasingly grown-up Asian power.

Father of the nation—after a shaky reputational period during New Order rule, Sukarno is back on top as Indonesia's number one historical hero.

History in Ruins

Much of Indonesia's architectural heritage is crumbling—especially the stuff from the colonial era. The port cities of Java's north coast—and other former Dutch outposts all over the country—are still home to large neighborhoods of colonial shop-houses, warehouses, and offices. But most of them are falling apart, red roof tiles sliding out of place, whitewashed walls mildewed to a grimy gray. The poignant air of decay makes the old quarters of Surabaya, Semarang, and similar cities wonderfully atmospheric places to explore—especially if you're a photographer. But they are a sorry contrast to neighboring Singapore and Malaysia, where many buildings from the same period have been scrubbed and saved for the tourists. There are signs of hope in the colonial Kota district of North Jakarta, however. A few years back it was a gritty, rundown neighborhood, but steps towards rehabilitation are underway, and the central Fatahillah Square is now something of a hipster hangout.

A derelict Dutch-era shop-house in the old city of Surabaya.

Obama in Indonesia

When Barack Obama was elected president of the United States there was a whole lot of excitement in Indonesia. While the rest of the world was celebrating the fact that he was America's first black president, Indonesians were more inclined to cheer the fact that he was America's first Indonesian president—well, sort of...

In 1967, a six-year-old Obama arrived in Indonesia with his mother and his Indonesian stepfather, Lolo Soetoro. The family settled in the South Jakarta suburb of Menteng, and the boy known as "Barry" went to a local, Indonesian-language school. By the time he went home to Hawaii in 1971, young Obama was a fluent Indonesian speaker with a penchant for the Indonesian meatball soup known as *bakso*. He seems to have forgotten most of his Indonesian these days, but everyone got very giddy when he managed a few words of the language during his first presidential visit to the country in 2010—and he was also, surely, the first international leader ever to be served bakso as part of a state banquet!

A PATCHWORK OF RELIGIONS

You might have heard that Indonesia is an "officially secular country", but that's not quite true. Pancasila, the national philosophy invented by Sukarno and promulgated by Suharto, makes the "belief in the one and only god" an essential part of Indonesian identity. Thing is, though, the phrase that Pancasila uses—Tuhan Yang Maha Esa—doesn't specify any particular religion. Indonesia might not be secular in the strictest sense, but when it comes to faith you certainly have options...

Muslim men at prayer.

For the purposes of form-filling and basic categorization, all Indonesians are expected to belong to one of six officially sanctioned religions. Sunni Islam amounts for by far the biggest chunk of the population, followed by Protestantism and Catholicism (in Indonesia, when people say they're "Christian", they mean they're Protestant; Catholics call themselves *Katolik*). Hinduism, Buddhism, and Confucianism bring up the rear. You

Badge of faith—a bumper sticker in Christian-majority Kupang.

might wonder exactly how being a Hindu—let alone being a Buddhist or Confucian—squares with "belief in the one and only god", but this is a classic piece of Indonesian compromise that works perfectly so long as no one asks too many searching questions!

Demographic percentages give a misleading impression of Indonesia's religious patchwork. Most of the Muslims are crammed into densely populated Java; Christianity dominates in large swaths of eastern Indonesia, and Hinduism accounts for the majority in Bali. And even in Muslim-majority regions, the religious minorities tend to be disproportionately represented in the cities, and in the ranks of the middle classes.

HOW RELIGIOUS ARE INDONESIANS?

Just how seriously does the average Indonesian take his or her religion? It's as impossible to make broad generalizations on this subject for Indonesia as it is for Britain or America. There are Muslims who never go to mosques and who know next to nothing about Islamic scripture; there are fundamentalist Protestants whose life is ruled by their faith; there are religiously chauvinistic Hindus, lapsed Catholics, proselytizing Buddhists, skeptical Confucians, and every other shade imaginable within the ranks of each of the six official religions.

But what's important is that virtually every Indonesian has at very least a nominal religious identity. If asked, almost everyone, young and old, will immediately self-identify as "Muslim", "Christian", "Catholic" or whatever it may be. This is partly down to official

A Javanese man meditates at an ancient Hindu temple near Blitar, centuries after the area converted to Islam.

and societal expectations, but also because the designation is often as important a part of identity as the practice. All Indonesians are supposed to list their religion on their official identity card, their KTP, and being a mere "KTP Muslim" or a "KTP Catholic" is better than being a nothing, because the one thing it's really *not* easy to be in Indonesia is a declared atheist.

Despite the official limitation to just six recognized religions, Indonesia has always been home to a huge array of local indigenous belief systems—from the *Kaharingan* of the Dayaks to the *Marapu* ancestor worship of Sumba. The state, however, has never recognized these traditions, and there's no

Religion by the Numbers

Muslims: 87.18 percent
Protestants: 6.96 percent
Catholics: 2.91 percent
Hindus: 1.69 percent
Buddhists: 0.72 percent
Confucianists: 0.05 percent
Other/Unrecorded: 0.49 percent

option to tick "other" when it comes to ID card applications or census forms, so over the decades most people have signed up, technically at least, for an official religion. In some cases adherents of a traditional belief system have successfully argued that their faith is a form of Hinduism. That's what many Kaharingan-practicing Dayaks have done. Elsewhere, there have been canny separations of the concepts of *agama* ("religion") and *adat* ("custom"). A great example of this is Tana Toraja in Sulawesi where most people are now happily practicing Protestants, even while enthusiastically continuing to take part in "customary" expressions of the older *Aluk Todolo* belief system.

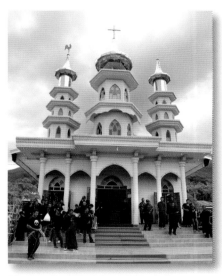

Churches in eastern Indonesia can be every bit as ostentatious as mosques in the western parts of the country.

Islam Nusantara and Kejawen

In books and travel articles, you'll often read of a supposedly distinct version of Islam in Indonesia—some sort of uniquely tolerant blend of Muslim belief, Hinduism, and animism. But there's a good deal of confusion, a number of different names, and a certain amount of nonsense bandied about when it comes to this topic.

One term that's become popular in recent years is Islam Nusantara. It means "Archipelago Islam", and in truth it's more of a modern brand than an actual religious tradition, something promoted by progressive Indonesian Muslim organizations, and those foreign journalists whose ears they catch, and representing what they regard as the Indonesian ideal of a mild version of Islam, thoroughly tolerant of other religions even if fairly orthodox itself. Quite separate is the far older entity known as Kejawen. This is the specifically Javanese traditional belief system

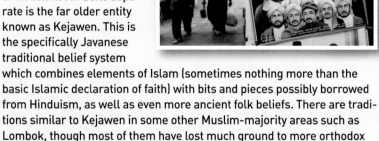

which combines elements of Islam (sometimes nothing more than the basic Islamic declaration of faith) with bits and pieces possibly borrowed from Hinduism, as well as even more ancient folk beliefs. There are traditions similar to Kejawen in some other Muslim-majority areas such as Lombok, though most of them have lost much ground to more orthodox interpretations of Islam in recent years—even if those more "modern" versions sometimes happily match the description of Islam Nusantara...

Being an Atheist in Indonesia

Any Indonesian who decides to "come out" as an atheist will have a tough time of it—from family, friends, and wider society. If they have an official role—as a teacher or civil servant, for example—their career may even be in danger. Even Indonesians who are otherwise paragons of religious tolerance—and even those who make absolutely no effort to practice their own faith—tend to find the idea of atheism hard to accept. This is partly because of a tendency for Indonesians to see a sinister association between atheism and communism, but it's mostly because religious designations are such an important part of identity. Not that Indonesian atheists don't exist—there are several Facebook groups where they offer one another support, and in recent years there's been a certain amount of unofficial tolerance of people leaving the "religion" section blank on forms and ID cards. For a moving insight into life as an Indonesian atheist, search online for a much-discussed essay on the Magdalene website by Aditya Nandiwardhana.

A SUPERNATURAL MENAGERIE: SPOOKY, CREEPY INDONESIA

You might not want to go out after dark in Indonesia. The whole country is positively crawling with things that go bump in the night. And what's more, modern pop culture and social media have done nothing to bust the ghosts; they've given them a whole new lease of life...

The Balinese demon-witch Rangda—one of the nastiest figures from classical mythology.

According to popular folklore Indonesia is home to a mindboggling menagerie of supernatural horrors in all shapes and sizes. The origins of the various creepy creatures are rich and varied. Some are probably Hindu or Buddhist figures, cut loose from their religious beginnings and set free to rampage in the darker reaches of popular imagination. Others are local place-spirits and pre-Islamic deities, gone rogue in the forests and abandoned buildings. And still others are just good old-fashioned bogeymen, designed to scare the children.

The general Indonesian word for ghost is *hantu*. You'll also hear talk of *jin*, the Islamic supernatural beings, as well as *setan*, "demons". But there are countless other more specific ghostly creatures too. There's a powerfully enduring idea, drawn from traditional belief systems, that a human spirit tends to hang around for a while after death; most of the officially sanctioned Indonesian religions manage, at a pinch, to accommodate this notion, and most people readily grasp the idea that such a spirit might turn nasty if not treated with respect. Many of the most popular ghost stories feature people who've died badly without being properly laid to rest.

Particularly gruesome are the legions of female ghosts, most notably the dreaded *kuntilanak*, the ghost of a woman who has died in childbirth. Kuntilanak tend to haunt lonely roads at night in the guise of a beautiful girl— and woe betide any man who tries to chat one up. Even more gruesome is the *sundel bolong*. A vengeful victim of rape and murder, she tends to look very alluring until she turns her back to reveal the gaping, bloodied hole in her rear torso. Then there's the *pocong*, which can be male or female, and which comes hopping—yes, *hopping*; not very scary, I know—out of the grave, still wrapped in its Muslim burial shroud. There's the *wewe gombel*, a grim old hag who

A Night in a Haunted Hotel

Every town in Indonesia has its haunted spots. Graveyards, old buildings, and especially old hospitals, are almost invariably considered haunted. The Jakarta History Museum on Fatahillah Square is said to be very thoroughly haunted by victims of colonial-era brutality. Another notoriously haunted spot is Hotel Niagara— an improbably salmon-pink hulk of art deco masonry on the road between Surabaya and Malang in East Java. It doesn't look much like the archetypal haunted house, but every time I passed it with Indonesian friends, they would shudder and avert their eyes. There were stories of rooms that filled with blood at night, and of the malevolent spirit of a Dutchwoman murdered in the hotel by Japanese soldiers during World War II. I was determined to investigate, so I decided to check in for the night. My friends in Surabaya thought I was crazy—not for chasing a ghost story, but for being brave enough to spend the night in such a creepy place. In the end I experienced nothing more than a disappointingly good night's sleep, but I did discover that the upper two stories of the hotel were mysteriously off-limits—perhaps that's where the bloody bedroom and the malingering Dutchwoman were to be found...

Left A young boy gets dressed up as a *pocong*.

Above and right Balinese monsters

makes a good job of frightening kids out of wandering away from home at night, plus the mischievous *tuyul*, a sort of skinhead goblin. If you can manage to tame a tuyul, it'll steal money and valuables at your behest and make you very rich indeed.

WITCHES AND SHAPESHIFTERS

As well as ghosts there's a widespread belief in mortal humans with dark supernatural powers. In Bali you'll hear tales of *leyak*, witches capable of shapeshifting, and with a penchant for drinking the blood of newborn babies. One Balinese friend insisted to me that he'd regularly seen a rider-less motorbike speeding along the lane outside his house on dark nights—a leyak with particularly modern shapeshifting skills. In Nusa Tenggara and Maluku there are similar figures known as *suangi*, and just about everywhere there are people reported to practice black magic. At its most modest level, the popular belief in the supernatural manifests in a nationwide passion for charms and blessings to provide either financial good fortune, or protection from physical harm.

Cinema and TV seem to have actually encouraged the Indonesian ghost craze, with an endless round of cheap horror movies hitting the screens. Sexy kuntilanak are a particular favorite of the Indonesian film industry. As for social media, I got bored long ago of people showing me supposedly genuine video footage of pocong on their mobile phones…

How **Not** to Teach an English Class!

When I was working as a language teacher in Surabaya, I found that ghosts often made for great teaching material. You could easily hang a whole bunch of tasty new vocabulary and lots of examples of English verb tenses on a ghost story. But sometimes it all went horribly wrong.

I once started a lesson with a group of teenagers by asking if any of them had ever seen a ghost. Most of the responses were pretty silly, but then I noticed that one normally talkative girl was behaving strangely, sitting silently with her head bowed. I asked if she'd ever seen a ghost, and she replied, "Sometimes." Oblivious to the rising tension in the room, I continued to prod her as to what she meant by this, even as she slouched ever lower in her chair, and her classmates edged towards hysteria. Eventually, in a spine-chilling "I see dead people" moment, I realized that her English was letting her down: she didn't mean "sometimes"; she meant "always"! She apparently had the common Indonesian gift of second sight.

"Can you see one now?" I asked, and my skin crawled as she nodded grimly and pointed up towards the ceiling, where, she explained, a pale-skinned female cyclops had been hovering since the start of the lesson. At this point I came to my senses and realized that we were the only people left in the room—the rest of the class had fled in terror. We had to finish the lesson in another classroom…

PULANG KAMPUNG: A NATION OF VILLAGES

So far in this book, we've mostly been looking at life in modern Indonesia—the world of malls and multiplexes, popstars, bloggers, and celebrities. And make no mistake, in the 21st century all that stuff is as "authentic" a version of Indonesia as any vision of temples and rice terraces. But of course, many foreign travelers—and these days a good number of city-dwelling Indonesians—want to experience an older, more "traditional" way of life as they explore the country. The good news is that the "traditional Indonesia" does still exist, often just a few steps sideways from the busiest city streets—just don't be surprised if its inhabitants all own mobile phones and have Facebook accounts!

Above The remote island of Sumba has some of Indonesia's most traditional village communities.
Below Family life in a traditional village in Sumba.

There's a well-worn cliché which claims that Indonesia is a "nation of villages". But while it's clichéd it is also, in many ways, true. The Indonesian word for "village", *desa*, actually comes originally from the Sanskrit term for "country", and the idea of "the village" is a very important one in Indonesian culture. For sure, being "villagey"—kampungan, or ndeso—is to be an unsophisticated laughing stock. But the village is also a focus of misty-eyed nostalgia, and a *gadis desa* is the kind of wholesome girl even the hippest urban fellow might fantasize about marrying in idle moments. Meanwhile, the attraction of *pulang kampung*, "going home to your village" for a visit after time spent living away, is something everyone understands, even if they've spent their whole life in a Jakarta apartment block!

Villages in Indonesia—and especially in Java and Bali—don't necessarily match up to the European notion of a compact huddle of houses surrounded by fields. A desa is often a sprawling area, with homes and small businesses strung out along a network of lanes across a very wide area. Within one of these large desa—which is a political unit with elected leaders, as well as a social one—you'll find individual *kampung* (or *banjar* in Bali), a term usually translated as "hamlet". A kampung is gener-

Five Traditional Villages to Visit

There are traditional villages all over Indonesia. These are some of the most striking and most accessible to outsiders. Some of them do make an income from tourism, but they are authentic communities nonetheless, and great starting points for off-the-beaten-track explorations nearby.

TENGANAN Probably the single most accessible "traditional village" in Indonesia, Tenganan, close to the resort of Candidasa in eastern Bali, gets hundreds of visitors every day, but it's still a deeply traditional community, with a strong sense of identity and a beautiful setting.

TARUNG Sumba in East Nusa Tenggara is my favorite place for exploring "traditional Indonesia". The whole island is speckled with deeply traditional communities, many of them rarely, if ever, visited by outsiders. The best introduction to this world is Kampung Tarung, a hilltop community of tall thatched houses right in the heart of Waikabubak, the main town in the west of the island.

KE'TE' KESU' Tana Toraja in Sulawesi has the most spectacular traditional architecture anywhere in Indonesia, with twin lines of lavishly decorated village homes with soaring rooflines. This community, a short drive from the main town of Rantepao, is one the most easily reached.

Above Spectacular funerals are a major feature of village life in Tana Toraja, Sulawesi.
Left Urban kampung kids.

ally a more compact community than the bigger *desa* to which it belongs, and it's here that you'll find the real vision of the village.

Of course, if you're looking to find the most obviously "traditional" villages, you'll generally need to head into the more remote parts of Indonesia. The province of East Nusa Tenggara, with its string of small, culturally distinct islands, is probably the best place in Indonesia for finding seriously photogenic traditional villages. Flores and Sumba in particular have a wealth of communities where striking wood-and-thatch architecture still dominates and old customs are observed.

Some are firmly on the tourist track, but there are dozens more besides. Another great place to find such communities—with even more dramatic architecture—is Tana Toraja in Sulawesi. It's important to remember, though, that these communities aren't living museums, insulated from the world of pop, punk, and the Internet that we've been exploring in this book. Don't be surprised for a minute if you hear an Agnes Monica ringtone echoing out from the gloom of a traditional village house in the green hills of Flores!

URBAN VILLAGES

Beyond their colonial or royal cores, most of the major urban centers in Indonesia grew up organically, outlying villages gradually swelling into a single, sprawling mass. It might not be obvious from the map, but outside of the central business districts and the most exclusive housing complexes and apartment blocks, the institution of the village survives in town. City neighborhoods are divided into administrative units called *kelurahan*, the urban equivalent of the desa, and in working class areas you'll find individual urban kampung within these units. These are usually ramshackle neighborhoods of beetling alleyways where life is lived out in the open and where the sense of community is strong. These urban kampung are easy to find, and easy to explore. The old colonial-era quarters of northern Jakarta, Surabaya, and Semarang are great places to wander, and in the outer Kraton quarters of Yogyakarta and Solo you'll find rather more prosperous traditional neighborhoods.

BENA South of the town of Bajawa in Flores, Bena has featured in countless Indonesian TV travel shows, but it's still one of the most visually striking traditional communities in the country, an elliptical ring of wooden houses in a stunning mountain setting.

BOTI Deep in the hills of West Timor near the town of Soe, Boti takes a lot more getting to than the other places in this list, and it's not, at first glance, as visually impressive. But it's a very special place indeed, a bona fide "kingdom" ruled by its own raja, with its own indigenous belief system. It is a place that's stayed aloof from the modern Indonesian state in many ways.

The village of Bena, in the lush green heart of Flores.

CRAFTSMEN, ARTISTS AND PERFORMERS

Indonesia has always had a serious reputation for arts and crafts—from elaborate performances rooted in mythology to intricate masterpieces in the medium of cloth—and you'll still find many of these traditional forms going strong today. But while most tourists come seeking nothing more than batik and wayang kulit, if you look a little deeper you'll also find one of the most vibrant, innovative—and indeed lucrative—modern arts scenes in Asia.

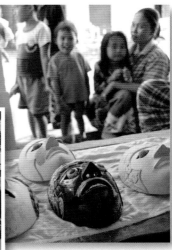

Above and left Intricate woodwork from Central Java.

The delicately filigreed leather puppets of the wayang kulit cast a very, very long shadow. This ancient form of performance art is pretty much an international symbol of Indonesia, invoked by every passing travel writer. But wayang is just the start of it.

Bali and Java are undoubtedly the sources of the most sophisticated and refined forms of traditional performance art. Many traditional dances have their origins in courtly and religious ritual. The *bedoyo* and *srimpi* dances of Central Java were originally functions of the royal Javanese palaces, and indeed the srimpi was originally only performed by actual princesses. In Bali, meanwhile—where the entertainment requirements of tourism have made sure that traditional performance arts have remained a very big thing—many dance-dramas double up as serious religious rituals. In fact, in both Bali and in remote corners of Java, some traditional dances cross the line from performance to possession—the forces of the supernatural get involved and take over the choreography, sometimes in quite terrifying fashion. That's the story, anyway…

PICKING UP THE THREADS

Next to wayang kulit, Indonesia's best-known artistic form has to be batik, the complex method of decorating cloth—either silk or cotton—by repeated dyeing while blocking out certain sections from the effects of each new color with intricate patterns of melted wax. The finest batik comes from Central Java (though I personally prefer the more colorful, creative versions from Madura and the ports along Java's north coast, where Chinese and other influences replace repetitive abstract patterns with birds and flowers). They do make batik in several other Asian countries, but don't mention that fact too loudly in Indonesia. The suggestion that batik might have been invented elsewhere gets people very cross—and the suggestion that it might have been invented in Malaysia is enough to start a riot!

The other classic textile form of Indonesia is *ikat*. It's a rougher, earthier tradition than batik, and to be honest, I find it much more appealing (even though I'm very happy to wear a batik shirt instead of a suit on formal occasions). Ikat is woven, with color patterns tie-dyed into the threads before they are put onto the loom. You'll find local varieties in every corner of the country, but the real ikat heartland is in the islands stretching eastwards from Bali.

Traditional crafts in wood and cloth: dance masks, carved in a village in Madura **(right)**; beautiful batik from the north coast of Java **(below)**; and an array of ikat from Nusa Tenggara **(left)**.

Wayang for Beginners

Everyone talks about wayang kulit, Indonesia's iconic tradition of shadow puppetry. Everyone recognizes the strikingly stylized outlines of the puppets themselves. And everyone knows that it is the country's most culturally significant performance art form. Even UNESCO thinks it's a "Masterpiece of Oral and Intangible Heritage of Humanity". But what the hell is wayang kulit all about? And is it actually worth watching?

Wayang is rooted in Java, and especially in Central Java, but there are sophisticated versions in Bali too, and minor local variants in several other corners of the country. The puppets, made of intricately filigreed buffalo hide, are wielded by the *dalang*, the puppet-master, a figure commanding enormous respect, and traditionally regarded as having borderline supernatural powers. The puppets are manipulated against a backlit cotton screen, with musical accompaniment from a gamelan orchestra. The stories told in wayang performances are usually drawn from the Indian epics, the Ramayana and the Mahabharata, but with all manner of Indonesian modifications and additions. The characters are divided into *alus* and *kasar* categories, the "refined" princely and heroic figures with their pointed noses and slender figures, and the chunky, "coarse" ogres and clowns. And that, I'm afraid to say, is about as far as the easily accessible aspects of wayang go.

A traditional performance features something like 50 different puppets, and lasts around nine hours, usually through the night; what's actually going on in the various scenes would be pretty obscure even if the narration wasn't all in high Javanese. And modern formal wayang performances in theatre settings tend to be robbed of all the near-mystical atmosphere that's supposed to be the main attraction. Suffice to say, this is not the most accessible art form for casually curious foreigners. If you do happen to come across an authentic, traditional wayang performance—which is always a possibility in Central Java—my advice is to focus on the wider spectacle, and the dreamy, smoky atmosphere. Have a look on the backstage side of the screen (this is perfectly permissible) where things are much more interesting. And don't for a minute feel obliged to stay until the end! If you do want to catch a truncated wayang showcase, the Wayang Museum on Fatahillah Square in Jakarta often puts on decent performances.

MODERN ART

When it comes to visual arts in the modern mediums of oil and canvas or ink and paper, it can sometimes be tough for foreign visitors to get past the tourist tat. In Bali in particular—supposedly the most artistic island in Indonesia, if not the universe—gift shops and commercial galleries are loaded with paintings that are often nothing more than luridly kitsch visions of rice terraces, or at best formulaic rehashes of the Wayang and Batuan styles, cooked up during collaborations between expat and local artists in the last decades of the colonial era. But none of this has anything to do with what's going on in the contemporary galleries of Yogyakarta and Jakarta—and indeed Bali, once you get off the Ubud main drag.

Yogyakarta, rather than Bali, is usually seen as the capital of Indonesia's serious, non-touristy, arts scene. The Indonesian Institute of the Arts is there; seminal figures in the development of contemporary art including Affandi and Hendra Gunawan were based there, and many of the current big names call the city home, even if their highest-profile shows are in Jakarta. Many of the biggest names in current contemporary art in Indonesia cut their teeth during the New Order years, and you'll often find unsettling threads of political satire running through their work. Heri Dono offers up disturbing images that look like snapshots from an LSD user's view of a wayang kulit show; Eko Nugroho does unsettling and intricate monochrome visions; and Nyoman Masriadi takes the political cartoon to its most surreal and sophisticated extreme. And these guys all command top dollar on the international art markets.

The streets are a space for artistic expression in urban Indonesia—accomplished graffiti in Jepara.

CHAPTER 7

INDONESIAN FOOD

There's so much more to Indonesian food than nasi goreng. The country is a chili-powered, coconut-scented, peanut-sprinkled gastronomic bonanza, as soon as you step beyond the tourist restaurants and the fast food joints. Want to know the difference between *tahu* and *tempe*, or between a *warteg* and a *kaki lima*? Trying to work out if *es dawet* is a drink or a dessert? Grab your fork and spoon (no knives and forks here), and tuck in...

MORE THAN JUST NASI GORENG: THE JOYS OF INDONESIAN CUISINE

If there's one thing that tops surfing, history, and punk rock in my personal list of geeky Indonesian obsessions, then it has to be food. And I'm not alone. Food—and talking about food—are national fixations, and the search for whatever's *enak* ("delicious") is the eternal Indonesian quest. And food is one of the few aspects of life where gengsi is routinely trumped by the inarguable fact of flavor. Sure, there are ranks of plush restaurants offering ersatz pizzas and pastas in every middle-sized city, but when it comes to seriously satisfying the taste buds, even the richest residents would still often prefer to chow down at some rickety wooden bench under the canvas of a side-of-the-road stall. People will regularly drive an hour or more just to eat at some particularly renowned chicken or noodle stall.

For some reason, Indonesian cuisine has always managed to travel just under the radar of international taste trends. Beyond the occasional nasi goreng or sate on the menus of pan-Asian restaurants, you'll struggle to find examples of it overseas. And when food journalists are tasked with listing "must-try" dishes from various countries, they inevitably name the afore-mentioned nasi goreng for Indonesia. Nasi goreng. Fried rice. Seriously, c'mon! From the fathomless dark depths of *rawon* or *rendang*, to the zinging-fresh hit of tamarind in a good *pecel* sauce; from the crunchy promise of a *martabak* sizzling in hot oil, to the delicate coconut-scented coolness of a *dadar gulung*; from the lurid, rainbow-colored ridiculousness of *es teler* to a delicate serving of *nasi Bali*, arranged like an offering on a round of banana leaves: there is a lot more to eat here than fried rice!

Part of the problem is that many foreign visitors to Indonesia simply

From top to bottom Padang-style sate with curry-flavored sauce, a Balinese mixed rice plate and a classic nasi goreng

Indonesia's Domestic Goddess

One day a few years back I was waiting for the lights to change at a pedestrian crossing on Singapore's Orchard Road when I happened to glance left at the rather stately woman standing next to me. I abruptly went weak at the knees as I realized that I was inches away from an authentic culinary superstar, queen of the Indonesian TV kitchen, and everyone's favorite "sexy chef". It was Farah Quinn. Born in Bandung in 1980, Quinn spent most of her teens and twenties in the USA, but in 2008 she came home to Indonesia to launch a career as a TV chef, and very rapidly became a household name. Detractors sneeringly claim that she's little more than a glamor model with a frying pan. But though her success might have a good deal to do with her looks, you can tell that she actually does know how to cook. She's a qualified pastry chef, and she served her time in hotel kitchens in the US before beginning her TV career. As for what happened on Orchard Road that day—I'm afraid I was too star-struck to speak; the lights changed, and the domestic goddess vanished into the crowd...

History, Food and Language

You can often trace the threads of culinary history, of distant foreign influences, and ancient trade links, in the language of food. The Indonesian words for butter and cheese, *mentega* and *keju*, are borrowed from Portuguese, suggesting that it was Iberian sailors who first introduced those substances to the archipelago. Meanwhile, the words for bread and wheat—*roti* and *gandum*—are of Indian origin, and it was almost certainly Indians who first brought wheat and its products to Indonesia. *Mie*, the word for noodles, along with the names for numerous individual dishes, come from Chinese, and there are various baked goods that have modified Dutch names. And the Indonesian word for "burger"? No prizes for guessing — it's burger!

don't engage properly with local cuisine. If you eat in tourist restaurants in Bali or Yogyakarta, you'll generally be faced with a menu on which only the inevitable nasi goreng and, if you're very lucky, some sort of generic curry do national service alongside the pasta carbonara and the margherita pizza. Little wonder, then, that many people come away thinking that Indonesian

food is pretty dull. What you have to do is get out there; dive in head first; *ask* people. Not only every island, but every city has its own distinctive dishes, so whenever you arrive somewhere new, simply ask the first local you meet what food is particularly *khas*—"special"—to this place, and where's the best place to find it. There's no better Indonesian conversation starter.

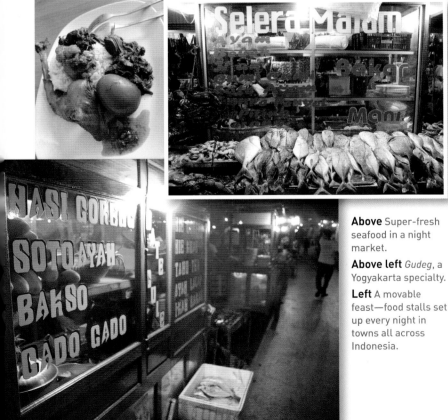

Above Super-fresh seafood in a night market.

Above left *Gudeg*, a Yogyakarta specialty.

Left A movable feast—food stalls set up every night in towns all across Indonesia.

Nasi Tumpeng: The "National Dish"

In 2013 the Ministry of Tourism and the Creative Economy was given an impossible task: to identify an official "Indonesian national dish". In a nation where every region has a multitude of local specialties, they must have wondered where to begin. In the end they went for *nasi tumpeng*, which is more a ceremonial event than a meal. Nasi tumpeng is only prepared for special events. It features an enormous cone of rice—either plain, or cooked with turmeric or coconut—symbolizing the volcanoes that have long had a role in traditional Indonesian belief systems. Around the bottom of this edible mountain are ranged various meat and vegetable dishes. Nasi tumpeng originates in Java, where it is still served in village *slametan*—thanksgiving ceremonies in which participants offer a nod to the ancestors. At the start of a slametan, the top of the rice cone is chopped off and served to the most important person present. To be fair, nasi tumpeng was a reasonable candidate for a pan-Indonesian dish, as it has long since spread from Java to all corners of the nation, and it appears at most important events such as the opening of a new business or a graduation ceremony. I had one prepared in my honor on my last day of work when I left my teaching job.

COOKING UP A STORM:
BAKAR, KUKUS, GORENG, REBUS

Long ago, before I put down the pans and took up the pen, I was a professional chef, and when I first arrived in Indonesia I came looking for new tastes and new techniques. But I have to admit that as someone with traditional European culinary training, my first reaction was something along the lines of "What the hell are you doing???" So much of it seemed plain wrong. Meat tossed into stocks and broths without being sealed first; astringent things like onions and garlic used raw in sauces; and everything cooked for what seemed like far, far too long—and then served at room temperature. But once I'd stopped looking and started tasting, I quickly forgot everything I'd learnt at chef school and realized that received culinary wisdom isn't always universal. After all, the king of Indonesian meat dishes, the mighty *rendang*, would count as an irredeemably overcooked beef stew with most European chefs. But what do they know!

Chili and Peanuts: The Columbian Connection

Indonesian cuisine would be a very different thing today if not for the arrival of ships bearing Iberian traders, some 500 years ago. Two of the most important of all ingredients in the archipelago—chili and peanuts—came originally from South America, and were first introduced to Asia by the Portuguese and Spanish, as were potatoes and papayas.

GOING WITH THE GRAIN

Indonesia, like most of its Asian neighbors, has rice at the heart of most of its cuisine. Rice is the ultimate staple food in all but the poorest regions of the east where cassava, sago, and other less nutritious starches take over. The rice grown and eaten in Indonesia is mostly of a long-grain variety, similar to what you'll find in Thailand and Vietnam (though glutinous rice is also sometimes used for desserts and sticky side dishes). It's usually served up steamed plain, but you'll also find it cooked with turmeric for an earthy yellow aroma, or as *uduk*—with coconut milk, which is absolutely delicious. But rice is really just the foundation for all sorts of other good things, cooked up in various different fashions.

TECHNIQUES AND INGREDIENTS

Though *bakar*—barbequing over charcoal—is a common cooking technique for street food, and a favorite manner of preparing fish, and while *kukus*, "steaming", is an important method for rice and some snacks and side

Goreng—a quick stir-fry is one of the two main Indonesian cooking techniques.

Above Cooking up a classic— nasi goreng, fried fast and hot in a wok.

dishes, the bulk of Indonesian cooking is by one of two techniques—hot and fast, or long and slow. There's *goreng*, frying in a heavy wok with a lavish quantity of oil—enough to blur the distinction between sautéing and deep frying—or *rebus*, stewing over a low flame. And occasionally the two are combined, as in the case of rendang, which starts with a fry, segues into a very long stewing, and then ends with another built-in fry.

Flavor foundation for many dishes, regardless of the cooking method, comes from *bumbu*—the wet spice grinds, not dissimilar to Thai curry pastes, which are essential in Indonesian cooking. There are infinite varieties of *bumbu* for infinite purposes, but core ingredients often include ginger and galangal, lemongrass, garlic, and vast quantities of shallots. Pestles and mortars are also

Tahu and Tempe

Indonesia isn't exactly a vegetarian's paradise, but it is home to two fabulous staples for non-meat-eaters: *tahu* and *tempe*. Tahu is simply tofu, white soybean curd, not here a New Age-ish alternative, but an everyday foodstuff. Tahu was probably introduced to Indonesia by Chinese traders many hundreds of years ago, but there's another soybean product which is indigenous to the archipelago, and which, as far as I'm concerned, is much tastier: tempe (sometimes also spelt tempeh). Unlike tofu, tempe is made from whole soybeans instead of curds, fermented and formed into blocks. It's meaty and nutty, and very high in protein, and it's absolutely delicious, especially when deep-fried.

Above Humble street side eateries like this one in Madiun, East Java, can sometimes have nationwide renown.

Left "Ayo, makan!" An invitation to eat on the streets of Indonesia.

Below Fresh fruits at the roadside.

used to create the cold sauces and condiments that are often where the real color—and the real fire—of Indonesian cuisine lies, the fierce, chili-powered sambals, and the cooler, peanut based sauces for dressing salads and sate.

A FRUITY FANTASIA

One of the simplest pleasures of eating in Indonesia comes from the wealth of tropical fruits. Sure, there are plenty of bananas, melons, mangos, all tasting a million times better than back home, having had a good deal more time in the sun before ending up in the market. But there's much more besides. *Manggis* (mangosteen) are small, hard, purplish fruits, but when you force your thumb through the thick rind you'll find segments of sweet, silky white flesh within. The unmistakably hairy red-green *rambutan* are something like a lychee though not quite as fragrant, while *langsat*, also known as *duku*, look like bunches of tiny potatoes and

The Daily Grind: Bumbu As a Way of Life

The most important piece of equipment in any Indonesian kitchen is a *cobek dan ulekan*, a pestle and mortar. This is where the real culinary alchemy takes place, in the creation of *bumbu*, the spice blends that are at the heart of Indonesian cooking, and of fiery sambal sauces. Unlike the versions usually found elsewhere, an Indonesian pestle and mortar does not feature a deep bowl and a straight grinder. Instead, the cobek is a wide, shallow stone plate, and the handle of the ulekan is crooked at a near-right-angle. The moment you first use one you'll realize how fundamentally flawed the design of those sold in kitchen shops back home really is. With the Indonesian version there's no exhausting pounding; instead there's a smooth, rhythmic back-and-forth motion that effortlessly turns shallots, ginger, and chili into a smooth paste in mere moments.

taste like a cross between a lychee and a lemon. *Salak*—usually called snake fruit in English—are the shape of a small pear and have scaly brown skin and crisp whitish flesh which tastes like a very dry apple. I'm never sure if I actually like salak—but I've eaten many kilos of them in the attempt to work it out! *Nangka*, jackfruit, is the biggest and ugliest of all fruits, great lumpen, knobby green things, but very tasty when ripe, vaguely custard flavored. It also makes a good ingredient in curries. I can't get away without mentioning the most notorious of Indonesian fruits, the durian. Now, I'll admit that I'm horribly prejudiced against durian, but as far as I'm concerned the fact that it looks more like a medieval implement of torture than a fruit tells you all you need to know!

Rice, by Any Other Name...

Rice is important stuff in Indonesia, so it's not surprising that there are some fine distinctions when it comes to what to call it. The cooked stuff on your plate is nasi; but when it's still dry and raw it's called *beras*. As for rice that's still growing, that's *padi*, which is where we get the term "paddy field"—though to make things even more confusing, in Indonesian a field where rice grows is called *sawah*!

Only in Indonesia: Hard-to-Find Ingredients

If you're trying out Indonesian recipes at home, you might find yourself looking for ingredients that even a specialist Asian supermarket will struggle to supply. Fortunately, most of them can be replaced with more readily available stand-ins without spoiling the overall effect.

Asam The Indonesian word for tamarind, asam, also simply means "sour", and tamarind is a vital souring agent in many dishes. Though it's not ideal, you can just about get away with using lime juice instead.

Tamarind

Kemiri Called candlenuts in English, I personally think these do more as a thickening agent than a flavoring. If you can't get hold of any you can always substitute cashews or macadamias—or leave them out altogether.

Candlenuts

Keluwak This one's a non-starter, I'm afraid. These nuts, essential for making the black beef stew known as Rawon, are nigh-on impossible to find outside of Southeast Asia (possibly something to do with the fact that they're highly toxic prior to the lengthy preparation process), and I've never managed to figure out a suitable alternative ingredient.

Keluwak Nuts (for Rawon)

Laos Known as galangal, or occasionally as "Thai ginger", in English, the flavor of this lumpy root is slightly sharper, but you can still get away with substituting regular ginger (*jahe*), even if the recipe calls for both laos and jahe.

Galangal Root

Terasi For something so pungent on its own, the effect of a small sprinkling of this fermented shrimp paste is remarkably subtle. You'll get a similarly fishy, salty effect from using Vietnamese-style fish sauce, which is usually easy to find in Western supermarkets.

Shrimp Paste

Sticky and Sweet **Kecap Manis, the Essential Condiment**

Along with the rest of the world, Indonesia inherited soy sauce—that black, salty liquid made from fermented soybeans—from China at some point in the distant past. But then local cooks decided to give it a unique twist all of their own: they mixed it with palm sugar to create something with the consistency of treacle, and almost as sweet. The resultant kecap manis—"sweet ketchup"—is the essential Indonesian condiment, and there's a bottle of it on every warung table in the country. It's good stuff; the malty, meaty soy flavor is still there, but with new nutty sweetness from the palm sugar. As well as a condiment, kecap manis is used as an ingredient in its own right, and adding a dash of it to any dish always gives it an unmistakably "Indonesian" flavor. The seasoning for the most basic nasi goreng is nothing more than equal squirts of kecap manis and bottled tomato sauce.

FOOD FOR THE PEOPLE:
EATING ON THE STREET

Indonesia is a nation designed for eating out. On every country road, on every roaring city thoroughfare, and on every beetling back alley there are eateries. They might be echoing, strip-lit dining halls where hundreds of hungry folks are served with military efficiency; they might be plush "restos" where the indolently rich edge themselves ever closer to morbid obesity; they might be ramshackle street-side spaces with sticky tables and concrete floors; or they might be nothing more than a wobbly wooden bench and a few plastic stools under a flapping canvas awning. But they're all flavor adventures. And even if there isn't a food outlet in sight, all you need to do is wait a few minutes and chances are you'll hear the approaching tock-tock-tock of a wandering bakso-seller, signaling his approach by tapping a spoon on an old bowl...

Above Fresh fruits waiting to be diced for a spicy rujak salad on the street.
Left On the go—A kaki lima stocked with bakso, the commonest street eat.

Apart from in the deepest countryside, Indonesians generally cook for themselves less often than most people in Europe or America. Even people with limited economic resources—especially those living in boarding houses—sometimes buy cooked meals seven days a week. The catering economy is designed for this, with the enormous array of budget eateries pitched and priced, not at the level of occasional indulgence, but at that of daily necessity, all of which makes Indonesia the greatest place on earth to indulge a taste for culinary adventure, and a sense of laziness in your own kitchen!

Very often you'll be sitting in an Indonesian home, everyone happily relaxed and settled in for the evening, sinetron on the TV, maybe even food on the table for later, and suddenly someone will casually say, "Anyone want to eat *mie ayam*?"—or fried duck, or rawon, or sate or whatever it may be—and 20 minutes later you'll all be clambering out of the car at some distant tented food stall...

EATERIES HIGH AND LOW

Indonesian eateries are strung along a long ladder of categories. At the top are the modern, international- and high-end Chinese-style restaurants, often called "restos", that you'll find in glitzy malls, inside upmarket hotels,

and along the flashiest city streets. To be honest, they're rarely exciting. I'd argue that the culinary interest factor often increases as the pricing decreases. Next step down the ladder are *rumah makan*, literally "eating houses", which are more traditional restaurants, generally with thoroughly functional décor. Padang restaurants typically fall into the rumah makan bracket.

At exactly what point a rumah makan becomes a *warung* is a mystery that

science has yet to solve. Some people suggest that if it's got proper windows, concrete walls, and a lockable door, it's a rumah makan, and if it's basically a temporary structure it's a warung. It's not perfect, but it's just about works as a definition—except in the case of *warteg*—short for *warung Tegal*—which do often have doors and windows! At a glance you might mistake a warteg for a Padang restaurant. There'll be a similar buffet-style array of cooked dishes in a glass cabinet out front. But the cuisine on offer is not from West Sumatra; instead it's a general mix of pan-Indonesian veggie and meat dishes (Tegal is a town in Central Java, but warteg food isn't really specifically Javanese).

When a warung's grip on a patch of roadside real estate slips altogether, you have reached the rung of the *kaki lima*—the food cart. Kaki lima means "five feet", supposedly referring to the three wheels of the typical cart, and the two legs of the vendor. Some—especially those offering bakso—are properly mobile, while others stake a claim to a fixed patch of pavement and come with a tarp for shelter and benches for diners.

Right At any transport hub you'll find stalls like this one stacked with fruits, soft drinks and packet snacks. They usually also serve *nasi bungkus*—simple packed lunches of rice and veggies wrapped in paper.

The eatery ladder doesn't stop there though—right at the bottom (though not necessarily when it comes to the tastiness of the wares) are the *bakul* ladies whose kitchen and larder is nothing more than a portable basket, and who you'll find throwing together snacks and small meals in most traditional markets. The humblest and most utilitarian of warung might serve a few unimaginative standards—nasi and *mie goreng*, and maybe *mie kuah* (instant noodle soup), plus a few trays of cold *gorengan* (deep-fried snacks), tea and coffee, and a colorful bank of packet chips, biscuits, and soft drinks. But the places that get the gastronomes going generally serve only one or two specialty dishes, and throw all their energy into serving them well. These are the places that people drive miles to dine at.

EATING LIKE AN INDONESIAN

In Indonesia the fork and the spoon, the *garpu* and *sendok*, reign supreme. You hold the spoon in your right hand, and eat with that; the fork is for shoveling food from the plate onto the spoon. Unless you eat out in a fancy restaurant serving Western food, you won't find knives on the table—and they're not really necessary as most Indonesian food comes already broken down into bite-sized pieces. Chopsticks only ever show up in places serving Chinese cuisine, and I've got quite a few Indonesian friends who can't use them and always have to ask for a spoon and fork if we eat Chinese. At home, and in certain types of eateries, people quite often eat with their hands. This is especially the case in the side-of-the-road warungs where they serve fried chicken, duck, or fish with rice and *lalapan* veggies. There will usually be a little bowl of water provided for you to clean your fingers before and after eating (as in pretty much every Asian country, you're not supposed to use your left hand for eating). Indonesian rice is quite starchy, and it's usually steamed for a long time, so it's sticky enough to make eating by hand easy, though you can always ask for a fork and spoon

Bakso

This is the most ubiquitous form of street food in all Indonesia. It's what Barack Obama used to eat when he was a kid in Jakarta, and when all else fails, on the remotest of mountain roads, there'll generally be a bakso seller somewhere to be found. It's a basic noodle and meatball soup, with a clear broth and a sprinkle of deep-fried onion flakes on top. To be fair, bad bakso is pretty miserable, and many a time I've found myself sitting waiting for a ferry on some lonely Nusa Tenggara dockside, staring glumly into a bowl of tepid gray liquid and rubbery lumps. But when you run into a good one, you can understand why a US president might think fondly of the stuff.

Snacks to Fry For

The name simply means "fried things", so you know that *gorengan* won't do much for your cholesterol levels, but they're just so good! Gorengan vendors fry up their wares on the spot in a big bubbling wok of hot oil. They usually sell an array of sweet and savory bite-size snacks, and you can get a pick-and-mix bagful for a few thousand rupiah. Classic gorengan include *pisang goreng* (banana fritters) and *pisang molen* (banana chunks wrapped in a strip of thin pastry). You'll also find cubes of fried tahu, either plain or *isi* (stuffed with shredded veggies and glass noodles), plus thin slices of ultra-crispy deep-fried tempe, and all sorts of *bakwan*—vegetable fritters very much like Indian pakora; *bakwan jagung*, made of sweetcorn, is my favorite.

Classic Street Eats: Martabak

This is my very favorite lapse into calorific evil, an oily-fingered indulgence on many a dark night on the road. It's also a dish that showcases the theatre of street food at its finest. Martabak is basically a very thin fried Indian-style bread, folded around a filling of egg, diced meat, and chopped scallions. They're always cooked on the spot, with the vendor whipping the dough out to paper-thinness on an oiled board before laying it delicately onto a sizzling hotplate. Martabak is generally meant to be taken home, but I'd suggest eating it on the spot—it tends to go soggy if wrapped up. Martabak stalls often dish up a coronary-inducing double act, the savory dish coupled with the dessert known as *terang bulan* ("bright moon") or *martabak manis* ("sweet martabak"). It's basically a North American-style pancake blown up to the size of a dinner plate and cooked on a griddle then folded over to make a two-inch-thick sandwich filled with chocolate, butter, sugar, condensed milk, cheese, peanuts, and whatever else you want to add.

if you're struggling. People tend not to linger over restaurant meals in Indonesia. Once everyone's finished eating, it's generally up, out, and on to the next destination without any long bout of small talk over the empty plates. In fact, it's one of the few circumstances that Indonesians *don't* routinely turn into an opportunity for endless conversation! This is probably because sitting together to eat around a table at a fixed time isn't normal behavior at home for most families: home-cooked food is usually just left out on the table all day under a fly-cover, and people eat whenever they feel hungry, without waiting for others to join them.

Above Cooking as street theatre—martabak (stuffed savory pancakes) on the griddle.

Left A roadside warung.

Left below Sundanese fried pigeon.

Below Pecel with a mighty array of add-ons from a cheery pavement vendor.

A THOUSAND ISLANDS, A THOUSAND FLAVORS

In a country that spans more than 3,000 miles, end to end, you'd expect to find at least a bit of regional variation when it comes to food. And yes, indeed: just like those other Asian mega-states, India and China, Indonesia has both a huge diversity of distinct regional cuisines, and certain indefinable continuities that make it all somehow "Indonesian".

This is a horrible generalization, and people from eastern Indonesia won't forgive me for saying it, but very roughly speaking the food in western part of the archipelago—basically Sumatra, Java, and Bali—is more sophisticated and complex than what you'll find in the east. These are the places where foreign influences were more often felt, and where ingredients, techniques, and flavors from China, India, Arabia, and beyond have been added to the melting pot of local cuisine. And these are also the places that have always enjoyed the greatest wealth and the richest agricultural bounties, and where the markets have always had a broader array of ingredients on sale. But if you thought that Java, long the cultural and political lodestone of the archipelago, would be the place that had the biggest impact in defining a general "Indonesian" style of food, then think again—the true queen of cuisines comes from the rugged western reaches of Sumatra.

PADANG: QUEEN OF CUISINES

The young men of the Minangkabau region of Sumatra, centered on the hills inland from Padang, have a long tradition of *merantau*—migration for work. In a happy twist of fate, they also happen to have the most gloriously rich and varied individual cuisine in the country, and this lucky combination means that there are *Masakan Padang* ("Padang Cuisine") eateries absolutely everywhere in Indonesia, from small roadside warungs in Nusa Tenggara, to lavish palace restaurants, designed like

traditional Minangkabau houses with flaming roof gables, in Jakarta.

The key feature of Padang cooking is variety. You get a big bowl of steamed rice, and then an almost infinite choice of side dishes from a bank of bowls, usually displayed behind glass at the front of the dining hall. In a more basic place you go up and point at what you want and get your plate preloaded, but in more upmarket restaurants a dozen or more small bowls are brought directly to your table. You only pay for what you eat, but once you've dipped into a

Above **A tantalizing array of Padang dishes.**
Above Inset **Gudeg**
Top **Popular Padang food stalls in Indonesia.**
Right **The kitchen crew.**

bowl, it'll go on the bill, so you need to choose without sampling. The key dish is rendang, that celebrated, slow-cooked beef or buffalo meat dry curry, but along with it you'll have a whole range of *gulai*—red or green coconut curries featuring fish, chicken, or various slightly alarming bits of cows. *Daun ubi*, cassava leaves, are the main green, but there are other veggie dishes too, including my favorite, *terong balado*, eggplant cooked with chili to a creamy softness, and there's always some very fierce chili sambal on the side.

JAVA; SPICE AND SWEETNESS

There's no single cuisine covering the whole of Java. This densely populated, agriculturally bountiful, trade-saturated island has countless local styles and specialties. In the west there's the Betawi cuisine of Jakarta—classic dish is *soto Betawi*, a tangy coconut and beef soup with a side order of rice and *emping* crackers. Then there's Sundanese cooking, which comes heavy on the fresh greens, often eaten *lalapan*-style, raw with sambal for dipping, and with the finest *tahu* in Indonesia. Once you cross from Sunda country into the Javanese-speaking heartlands, there's a whole new array of cooking styles. Very, very roughly speaking the food of south-Central Java around Yogyakarta tends to be heavily sweetened with palm sugar (the archetypal dish is *gudeg*—a very slow-stewed jackfruit curry, served with egg and beef crackling), while that of East Java is earthier, more savory, and with a stronger hit of chili. Rawon—a black beef stew, colored and flavored with keluwak nuts—is my Surabaya favorite.

Going Crackers

It's not a proper Indonesian meal unless it has a bit of crunch—and that crunch comes from the crackers. Known generically as *krupuk*, there are infinite varieties of crispy, crunchy things, including fish-and-prawn-flavored crackers, some made from rice starch, some from beef crackling, some big, some small. Crackers are an integral part of some dishes, such as *gado-gado*, and a good nasi goreng often comes with a handful of small ones. But any eatery worth its salt will also have crackers on the table along with the sambal and the kecap manis—they're not free, so you'll need to keep count of how many you eat before paying the bill. The most universal form

are *krupuk kampung*—big, squiggly cassava-flour crackers, that are usually stored in blue or red, glass-fronted tins.

Above The cracker man—a krupuk vendor making his rounds.
Left Freshly fried krupuk are available in a rainbow of colors.

BALI AND BEYOND

Bali might have a rich diversity of local dishes, but as far as the rest of Indonesia is concerned it's famous for one thing only—pigs! Fat, juicy, spice-marinated, spit-roasted pigs! In a country where Muslim food rules mean that pig flesh is *haram*—"forbidden"—for most of the population, the pork-guzzling tendencies of the Hindu-majority Balinese are always going to get a bit of attention. And for a few Javanese friends

Noodle Nation

Though noodles have probably been around in Indonesia since the first Chinese settlers arrived, many centuries ago, they were never very popular. But in the late 1960s, as the authorities battled shortages, Indonesia was obliged to accept food aid in the form of imported wheat, which begged the question: what to do with the stuff, and how to make people eat it? The answer was instant noodles. Through a combination of hyper-efficient production, aggressive marketing, and bargain-basement prices, packet noodles from brands like Indomie soon became a nationwide fallback staple, so entrenched in the Indonesian diet that even when the economy and the rice supply recovered they remained ubiquitous. The statistics say it all: in 1966 per capita wheat consumption was a mere 0.3kg; by 2010 it was a staggering 18kg—and much of that in the form of instant noodles!

Dining at The Outer Limits: Extreme Cuisine

Indonesia is not, for the most part, one of those "countries where they eat weird stuff". But if you step off the culinary Main Street with its abundance of chicken, beef, and fish, you can still stumble into wild territory. For Muslims, dogs are as far beyond the culinary palate as pigs, but Indonesia is a religiously diverse place and though it's never a mainstream meat, dogs do end up on the dinner plate here. It's served in the Batak regions of North Sumatra, in Timor, and in Manado in Sulawesi (which is regarded by most Indonesians as the ultimate culinary outland—not only dogs, but also rats, bats, and snakes all get served up there). They also eat quite a lot of dogs in Bali, though it never features in the tourist restaurants! Dog meat is most typically prepared as sate, and referred to as "RW" or "B1"—the Manado and Batak euphemisms—and if you search really hard you'll occasionally find it in served to Batak, Manadonese, and Balinese migrants in Jakarta, Surabaya, and other big cities nationwide. Personally I don't have any moral qualms about eating dog—it just doesn't taste all that good. But I would definitely balk at another meat that still occasionally gets surreptitiously served up in Bali—turtle. They're very rare, and protected by law, so folks shouldn't really be turning them into sate! Endangered species and canine companions aside, the average weak-stomached traveler is more likely to be freaked out by *soto Betawi* or *coto Makassar*—soupy beef stews featuring bits of the cow that would probably end up as dog food in Europe.

of mine, happy to commit culinary indiscretions when no one's looking, Balinese cuisine gets an extra dash of spice from its illicitness! The classic Balinese dish is *babi guling*, literally "rolled pig"—a spit-roast suckling pig in a heavy marinade of ginger, turmeric, garlic and more. The light, slightly sour spice tones of babi guling lack the earthier base notes of Javanese and Padang cuisine, and you'll find that same higher, more acidic quality in the flavoring of other classic Balinese dishes like *bebek betutu* (pit-roasted duck) and *pepes ikan* (fish steamed in banana leaves).

Once you start to island hop east of Bali the cooking tends to be a bit more pared down, and the spice starts to fade away—even, oddly, in Maluku, the original source of cloves and nutmeg. These places are generally poorer and drier, and even the paramountcy of rice begins to be challenged, with sago, cassava, corn, and sweet potato—traditionally poor man's starches—making their presence felt in home kitchens. Still, there are some treats here and there: *ayam Taliwang*, chili-marinated grilled chicken, named for a town in Sumbawa but more closely associated with neighboring Lombok; *coto Makassar*, a rich, hearty soup from Sulawesi (full of bovine "nasty bits", be warned). And wherever you are, even on the most distant specks of land at the furthest extremities of Indonesia, you can rest assured that there'll always be a Padang restaurant and a *sate Madura* stall…

Going Nuts For Nasi Pecel

I've never really been able to pinpoint my favorite Indonesian dish, but if I'm pushed hard I'll often say *nasi pecel*—there's just something about its zingy freshness that surpasses even the rich bounties of Padang cuisine or the moreish succulence of the best sate in Madura. It features a heap of steamed rice, blanched greens, fresh *selasih* (Asian basil), wonderfully crunchy *peyek* crackers, chicken, fried tempe or whatever takes your fancy, all topped with the most fabulous sauce—peanut based, but flavored with tamarind, kaffir lime leaves, chili and all sorts of secret ingredients.

Several towns, including Blitar and Ponorogo, claim it as their own, but the small East Java city of Madiun is the true pecel capital. I once ate eight portions in 24 hours there during a quest to find the very best version!

Sticking it to Them:
Madura's Sate-Selling Migrants

Sate—sometimes also spelt satay—might just be Indonesia's most successful contribution to world cuisine. Though Thailand and Malaysia sometimes try to claim it, miniature shish kebabs grilled over charcoal likely originated in Java (as far as Southeast Asia is concerned, anyway—the Javanese probably got the initial idea from Indian or Arab traders). There are all sorts of different sate varieties from all sorts of different places. There's sate Padang, which comes with a gloopy, curry-flavored sauce, and Balinese *sate lilit*, which is made from mince, kefta style. But there's no doubt that the commonest form of sate nationwide is that served up by the exiled chefs of Madura.

Dry, poor, and with thin limestone soils, migrants have been departing Madura's shores for centuries—and finding themselves the butt of bad jokes and even outright hostility in the process. Supposedly rough, tough, and coarsely spoken, migrant Madurese often suffer the same kind of suspicious distaste that met Irish laborers in England in the mid-20th century, or "Okies" in California a generation earlier. But when it comes to cuisine—and especially sate—the rest of Indonesia welcomes the Madurese with open arms. Sate Madura is generally made from goat or mutton, liberally salted, grilled hot and fast, and then served with diced shallots and a peanut sauce darkened with *kecap manis* and palm sugar, and with a side of *lontong* (rice steamed in banana leaves). You'll find Madurese sate stalls at roadsides all over the country.

Indonesia's Ultimate Acquired Taste

Dog sate and the nasty bits of cows, I can handle; but the one Indonesian food where I draw the line is a fruit—a big, spiky, smelly one. I'm talking about durian, claimed by some to be "the king of fruits", and claimed by me to be the work of the devil. They're green and covered with viciously sharp protrusions (the name means "thorny"), and they can grow as big as a football (don't confuse them with the bigger, less sharply-spiked, and much more pleasantly flavored jackfruit). Even before they're opened they give off a pungent, faintly industrial odor—something like diesel mixed with rotten eggs. The flesh inside is soggy and yellow. By no means do all Indonesians love durian, but those who do tend to wax lyrical about it. Be warned, durian also turns up as a flavoring in everything from biscuits to ice cream—and durian ice cream is probably the worst thing I've ever eaten in Indonesia! But who knows; you might be one of those people who actually like it...

THE WORLD OF INDONESIAN DRINKS: FROM KOPI TUBRUK TO BIR BINTANG

Is Java the best place to find a cup of java? Can you drink the tap water? Do they have beer in "the world's largest Muslim-majority nation"? And where exactly is the dividing line between a dessert and a drink? Welcome to the wonderful, frequently flamboyantly colored, and occasionally weird world of Indonesian beverages.

In Indonesia the world's two great caffeinated beverages go head to head for the status of "national drink". It's a hard call, but I think that tea just about takes it. It's what you're usually served—black, hot, sweet, and in a glass with a little metal or plastic lid to keep in the heat—when you visit someone's home. The coffee is pretty good too, though. It has been grown in Indonesia since the colonial era, and while less flavorsome Robusta varieties predominate, there are still pockets of the supreme Arabica. These days, the hipsters of Jakarta are all mad for their barista-style lattes, while truck drivers tend to go for "3 in 1" instant varieties. But as far as I'm concerned the proper way to drink coffee in Indonesia is old-school *kopi tubruk*—a solid inch of unfiltered grounds and a hefty spoonful of sugar dumped into a glass of hot water. The local coffee that ends up in *kopi tubruk* is pretty good in Java, but I think it's better in Bali, and better still in Sulawesi.

ES ET CETERA

Es teh manis—a glass of sweet black tea cooled by a big hunk of rapidly melting ice—is always my go-to drink for dining *a la* warung. But cold drinks in Indonesia frequently stray into much more peculiar territory. How about *es dawet*? It looks pretty much like a glass full of green worms. The wriggly things are actually pandanus-flavored rice-flour jellies, and you'll often find sweetened red beans in there too, all topped up with coconut milk. You need a straw *and* a spoon to finish a glass of the stuff. This half-drink, half-dessert theme has many other variations: *es cincau*, which comes with lumps of black jelly, and the infinite versions of *es campur*, "mixed ice", which is served in a bowl and is definitely more dessert than drink. It's a bit like a Hawaiian shaved ice, but with added weird jelly things as well

The Jamu Lady

If you're looking for a pick-me-up, keep an eye out for a lady with a basket full of bottles on her back—she's a seller of the murky traditional tonics known as *jamu*. You'll find jamu-vendors, usually middle-aged women of Javanese origin, all over Indonesia. There are also commercial producers of packet jamu— Nyonya Meneer and Djamu Djago are amongst the biggest brands. Jamu has its origins in ancient Javanese herbalism, with local leaves, fruits, and roots being key ingredients. But it also seems to owe something to traditional Chinese medicine, sharing the same notions of "heating" and "cooling" properties. As for what jamu actually does for your health, its fans will make all sorts of extravagant claims for its curative powers, but it seems most often to be taken as a general restorative against the vague malaise known as *masuk angin* (literally "entered by the wind")—either that or as *obat kuat*, a "strong medicine". I'm sure you can work which bit of you it's supposed to make "strong"...

The Most Expensive Coffee on Earth

It sounds like a joke, and a sick one at that: the most expensive coffee on earth is created from beans picked out of the droppings of a catlike creature known in Javanese as *luwak*, and in English as the palm civet. The animal's digestive juices supposedly do magical things to the coffee, and it sells for hundreds of dollars per kilo. Traditionally it was gathered from the ground in coffee plantations where wild civets lived, but these days it's often commercially produced from caged animals kept in horrible conditions. And here's the thing—quite a few serious coffee connoisseurs say there's nothing special about the taste. It could just be that kopi luwak really is a joke...

Gathering palm sap in Nusa Tenggara.

as a full rainbow of colored syrups. I love most of these Indonesian drink-desserts, but there's one thing I do draw the line at, and that's the perverse concoction known as *soda gembira*, "happy soda". It's made by mixing shocking pink syrup, condensed milk, and soda water, and there's nothing happy about that combination...

THE HARD STUFF

Indonesia might have more Muslims than any other country, but by no means do all of them abide by the Quranic prohibition on alcohol, and in any case, there are also millions of non-Muslim Indonesians with absolutely no religious inhibitions when it comes to having a quiet tipple. The mainstream Indonesian alcoholic drink is a very standard tropical pilsner beer, the kind found everywhere from Thailand to Mexico. There are various brands, including Anker and Bali Hai, but the ultimate beer in Indonesia is Bintang. There's nothing particularly special about it; it's just got overwhelming market dominance (helped by having multinational marketing and distribution clout behind it: it's owned by Heineken Asia Pacific). *Bintang* actually means "star", but it's also pretty much synonymous with "beer". It is to Indonesia what Guinness is to

Ireland... speaking of which, for some reason Indonesians also have a bit of a thing for Guinness, which is generally the only alternative to Bintang in the rougher sort of bars.

White Water

You can drink the water—just not out of the taps. The idea that water needs some kind of treatment before drinking is pretty much universal in Indonesia. Wealthy people get weekly deliveries of dispenser bottles from commercial suppliers such as Aqua. Those with a slightly tighter budget take the same bottles to a neighborhood depot where they're topped up with UV-filtered mains water. And those with even less to spend start the morning by boiling up a big aluminum kettle of tap- or well-water to see them through the day. All this counts as *air putih*, literally "white water", and you can be pretty confident that any water you're offered to drink—including that from the jugs on the tables in cheap warungs—will be safe.

Homebrew and Moonshine

Indonesia has a few good traditional homebrews, ranging from the pleasantly innocuous to the positively toxic. Of the former, the main variety is *tuak*, otherwise known as palm wine, and made by gathering sugary sap from either lontar or coconut palms and letting it ferment naturally. It's mild and slightly fizzy. You'll find it mainly in North Sumatra, and also the far east of Nusa Tenggara and Maluku where it is sometimes distilled and turned into something much harder called *sopi*. You'll also find moonshines made from rice, sugarcane, and other palm saps, including *lapen* and *ciu*, both from Java and both best avoided. The most palatable moonshine I've encountered was Lombok *brem*—a rice liquor with a faintly citrusy flavor.

The best known of all Indonesian traditional liquors is *arak*—which ranges in taste from cheap gin to diesel. It turns up on plenty of bar menus in the tourist areas of Bali and Lombok, but like all these homebrewed liquors it can be very, very dodgy, sometimes being tainted with anything from insecticide to methanol. Several tourists have died in Bali and Lombok in recent years after drinking arak.

CHAPTER 8

EXPLORING INDONESIA

Now you're primed with a bit of knowledge about what to listen to, what to watch, and what to eat, how could you not want to head out to explore the world's greatest archipelago? As a travel destination Indonesia has everything—from mountain summits to coral gardens, and from hedonistic party towns to lost villages on untrammeled islets. The going might be a bit tough at times if you head beyond Java and Bali, but the rewards are magnificent. It's time to *jalan-jalan*…

ISLAND-HOPPING ACROSS THE WORLD'S GREATEST ARCHIPELAGO

You only need to look at the map of Indonesia. That great arc of islands, threaded with roads like thin red veins, draws your eye ever onwards from landfall to landfall. You find yourself idly tracing a finger from Sumatra to Java to Bali and beyond, and suddenly you're lost in a wonderful whirl of "what ifs". What if I flew up there, and then traveled down here overland? I wonder if I could rent a motorbike here, and then head up into those mountains for a few days. Look at that little island—I wonder what it's like! There's probably a ferry from there...

Indonesia is a place that impels journeys, in the mind and on the ground. Surfer, history geek, sometime English teacher, sometime journalist, foodie, punk rocker, occasional sinetron watcher—all of those things take second place to the fact that when I'm in Indonesia, even if I'm stuck in an office, I'm really there as a traveler first and foremost. There have been countless journeys, from trans-Java motorbike jaunts to island-hopping odysseys in the outer limits of Nusa Tenggara, and from hikes through the misty uplands of Sulawesi to voyages on the dark rivers of eastern Sumatra, and I don't doubt for a moment that there will countless more before I'm done. In fact, I don't think I'll ever be done, and I can't see how anyone who ever sets foot in Indonesia—whether to live and work, or just as a passing visitor—could fail to be sucked into the archipelago's journey-inducing vortex. Just look at the map...

public transport going to that mountain town you've set your heart on, or that offshore island that's caught your imagination—it just might not be going today. Or tomorrow. In fact, no one really knows when it'll eventually depart, and even when it does, you can guarantee that it'll be *slow*. The massive expansion of budget air travel has certainly opened up outlying provinces which used to be weeks away from Bali and Java. But as soon as you set out beyond the dusty arrival halls of far-flung airports, things are often just as slow as they ever were.

But if you accept all this, and if you slow the pace between the long bouts of journeying, it's all part of the strange magic of Indonesian travel. That moment of eye-popping outrage when the bus pulls *back* into the Pekanbaru terminal, and you realize that for the past hour it's simply been trawling the suburbs for extra passengers and you're

Indonesia's traditional markets, such as these in Madura **(right)** and Central Java **(left)** are full of warm welcomes—though expect some good-natured haggling if you're looking to purchase anything.

no nearer to your destination than when you started, will seem funny two days later when you're dangling your toes in the cool clear waters of Danau Maninjau. That entire day you pass on a lonely jetty on the scorched northern shoreline of Sumba, with the answer to the question, "Is the ferry coming?" gradually shifting from definitely, to maybe, to definitely not, will take on a halcyon glow when you're back amongst the hordes in Bali. And those bowls of tepid gray bakso in gimcrack bus stands from Sabang to Merauke will seem like the finest appetizers for the fiery Padang-style feast laid out before you at dinnertime the following day.

THE ROUGH AND THE SMOOTH

You have to take the rough with the smooth when it comes to travel in Indonesia. In Java you can rattle to and fro on an excellent rail network, hail air-con taxis, and clamber onto plush coaches plying modern highways. And in Bali, if you so choose, you can be shuttled directly from guesthouse to guesthouse in pre-booked tourist minibuses. But once you pass out into the further reaches of the archipelago things sometimes get a bit trickier. There *will* always be some form of

Jalan-Jalan—On the Road

The word jalan means "road", and you'll see it everywhere on maps and signs, often abbreviated to "Jl." *Jalan Sudirman* is "Sudirman Street". But jalan is also the root for many Indonesian words relating to travel and movement, and it's used figuratively when looking back on a "journey"—in business, education, or in love. Jalan-jalan, meanwhile, means "wandering", "taking a walk"—and that can cover simply going out for a stroll around town, hitting the streets for a few hours on Saturday night, or embarking on a months-long island-hopping adventure.

Bule on a Bebek

Without a shadow of a doubt, I owe the greatest richness of my Indonesian travel experiences to that thing of wonder which is a step-through, 125cc Honda motorcycle, the mode of transport known in Indonesia as a *bebek*—literally a "duck". I'll admit, I was more than a little nervous when I first wobbled out onto the howling highways of Bali on a rented bike on my first visit; in fact, I was pretty much shaking in my sandals. But I've never looked back. Bikes have become so integral to my idea of travel in Indonesia that I can't really imagine life without them.

Living in Java I always had my own bike, and that was my instant means of escape come the weekend. While non-biking expats were still arguing with a taxi driver or bad-temperedly batting away ticket touts in a greasy bus terminal—or giving up and going to the mall instead—I was already somewhere out in the green, changing gear on the bend of a mountain road, looking for adventure. Elsewhere, my first question on disembarking a boat or a plane is always "Where can I rent a bike?" Without bikes there are numberless villages in the nether regions of Sumba, Flores, and Alor that I would never have visited, alone and without the need for driver or guide. There are infinite Balinese backroads, looking like colorized 1930s flashbacks, that I'd never have traversed, endless backwoods Javanese temples I'd never have stumbled upon, and limitless hours of happy conversation with chance-met strangers in bamboo warungs, out amongst the rice fields, that I'd never have had.

Traditional step-through bebeks are very easy to ride, and the fully automatic scooters that have become the in thing in the last few years even more so. There are organized rental places in major tourist destinations in Java, Bali,

Right Motorbiking in Indonesia is not without its challenges— this collapsed bridge in the mountains of Bali, for instance. Mind you, if I'd been in a car I'd have had to turn back!

and Lombok. And even far from the beaten track, you only need to ask around at a guesthouse and someone will always be able to sort you out with a bike for a few dollars a day.

Naturally, a first glimpse of the traffic on a highway in Bali or Java can be enough to convince first-timers that to climb onto a motorbike is to sign up for certain death. It's a perfectly understandable reaction; there certainly are risks involved; and I'm endlessly appalled at the sight of reckless young tourists blazing along the busiest roads in Bali as if they have a death wish. But even the busiest Indonesian traffic looks much less intimidating from the inside than from the outside. Chaotic it

Above and left Rural roads in much of Indonesia are a pleasure to ride, and with your own wheels you can stop for every photo opportunity.

might be, but it's never aggressive, and what's more, drivers of cars, trucks, and buses are far more "bike aware" than their counterparts in Britain. And most importantly of all, the vast, vast majority of Indonesian roads—even in crowded Java and Bali—look nothing like the howling highways you'll see from the bus or taxi window. Instead, they're tranquil strips of tarmac threading through field and forest—you'll just never get to explore them if you don't have your own set of wheels...

Five Must-Sees in Indonesia

BOROBUDUR AND PRAMBANAN Going to Java and not visiting these two epics of ancient stonemasonry would be like traveling to Cambodia and refusing to look at Angkor Wat, or going to Agra and not checking out the Taj Mahal.

GUNUNG BROMO You've seen the sunrise panorama from the Penanjakan viewpoint on a thousand postcards and in a hundred magazines, but no photo can match the direct experience of looking out over the cloud-filled Bromo-Tengger caldera in the clear light of an East Java dawn.

UBUD Long-term aficionados have taken to howling about how *Eat, Pray, Love* ruined everything, but it's telling that they're still there, sipping their organic wheatgrass shakes and striking their yoga poses. No matter how crowded it gets, Ubud will always be a town with a special kind of soul.

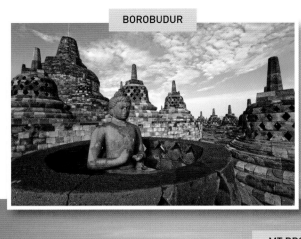

BOROBUDUR

MT BROMO

UBUD

TANA TORAJA Like a tropical version of the Shire from *Lord of the Rings*, with added buffalo sacrifices and wackier architecture, Toraja, in the green heart of South Sulawesi, is a very special sort of place.

KOMODO It used to take days of grueling overland travel to get to Labuanbajo, the gateway to the Komodo National Park. These days people fly straight in from Bali, and the once sleepy harbor village is a boomtown complete with luxury resorts. But out on the scorched offshore islands of Komodo and Rinca, the giant monitor lizards that started it all are still doing their thing, and under the surface there's some of Indonesia's finest diving.

TANA TORAJA

KOMODO

Five Off-The-Beaten-Track Adventures

GUNUNG PENANGGUNGAN Less than two hours south of central Surabaya, this small, perfectly formed mountain stands sentinel over the sweltering coastal flatlands. On its slopes, and sweeping up to the flanks of the larger Arjuno-Welirang range beyond, you'll find quiet lanes through rice terrace landscapes than make the best bits of Bali look plain by comparison—and all without a single tour bus in sight.

MADURA Most Indonesians will laugh if you mention Madura, but the area around Sumenep in the east of this much-maligned island is full of lazy charm and warm welcomes.

MADURA

DANAU RANAU Danau Toba, up in the north of Sumatra, gets all the traveler love, but this smaller lake, locked in amongst the ridges of the southern Bukit Barisan, is a very special sort of place, a million miles from beaten tracks.

NUSA PENIDA Who knew that a place like this could exist so close to the busiest bits of Bali? You can see it from the sea-view rooms of the beachfront hotels in Sanur, but this offshore limestone island is whole lifetimes away from brash resorts.

DANAU RANAU

NUSA PENIDA

SABU Beyond the furthest horizons and beyond the endmost pages of the guidebooks, there are whole galaxies of out-there islands to explore. This wildly remote lump of land at the outer limits of Nusa Tenggara is my personal favorite.

SABU

My Advice: Less is More

It's always the same when people tell me their Indonesia travel plans: "We want to see the orangutans in Sumatra; We definitely want to check out Borobudur, and we're going to do a bit of hiking in Tana Toraja, plus we *have* to see the Komodo dragons; I've always wanted to visit Borneo too—oh, and we're going to factor in some beach time in Bali at the end." And how long are you going for? "Three weeks..."

Indonesia spans a continent-sized surface area, and no one in their right mind would plot an itinerary like that in Europe or South America—and the transport in Indonesia is slower and less reliable than in those places! You could very, very easily spend a whole month of travel just in Java or Bali, and be on the go the whole time, seeing new places every day. Sumatra, Nusa Tenggara, or Maluku could easily suck up two months. And the thing is, you'll almost certainly have much more rewarding travel experiences that way. The alternative consists of endlessly dashing back to big, ugly cities to catch yet another interisland flight from yet another dreary airport. If you're coming to Indonesia for a month or less, then my advice is to put no more than two distinct areas on your itinerary: Java and Bali; Bali and Nusa Tenggara; Java and Sulawesi; you get the idea. You wanted to see more of Indonesia than that? Well, you'll just have to come back for a second visit...

INCOMPARABLE JAVA

Java. The name alone is enough to send a tingle down my spine. This is the part of Indonesia that I know best, and over the years it's completely seduced me with its strange dark magic, its volcano-haunted horizons, and its potent mix of noisy mayhem, sophistication, simplicity, and soft green silence.

But what saddens me is that so few of the thousands of travelers who visit Java each year see more than a tiny part of it. Most people come hustling through at a helter-skelter pace, going from Jakarta to Yogyakarta in one hit, doing a whistle-stop tour of the temples, then blazing on to Bromo for a sunrise selfie, and never slowing the pace for a moment until they reach Bali. Look at the map, for crying out loud! Java is ten times the size of Bali! It deserves a little more time!

Of course, to truly get beneath the green skin of Java, you need to break away from the big cities and the main highways, and get onto the country roads—and the simplest way to do that is with your own transport. But even if you're not willing to tackle the traffic and the navigation under your own steam, do yourself a favor and slow the pace at least enough to spend a night or two somewhere off the main trail—one of the out-of-the-way mountain towns like Tawangmanggu, or an East Java backwater such as Blitar or Pacitan. If you do that you might realize that there's no need to hurry on to Bali.

JAKARTA: ULTIMATE MEGACITY

There's no two ways about it: the Indonesian capital is one ugly monster of a city, sprawling interminably in a toll road-tangled mess, south, east, and west of its old core. By day there's a sickly, yellowish tint to the light, and as evening draws in there's a dark satanic quality to the skyline. It's certainly not the prettiest port of entry for an Indonesian journey, but there's no need to flee in terror: Jakarta is one of the friendliest megacities around. It doesn't have much by way of conventional tourist attractions, but if you end up

Java is the most modern part of Indonesia, but it also has powerful currents of tradition, from refined courtly customs in Yogyakarta (above top) to earthy village ceremonies (above bottom).

hanging around for a while and making some local friends, then limitless worlds open up—everything from cutting-edge art galleries to underground rock shows. And if you're just passing through en route for greener, calmer places, at least give yourself time to look around. The most interesting part of town for travelers is actually a fairly compact area—a two-mile strip stretching from Lapangan Merdeka, the vast ceremonial square at the core of the city, to the old port area at Sunda Kelapa. If you go to just one place within this area, make it Fatahillah Square in the Kota district. Steps are being taken to rehabilitate the surrounding colonial architecture, and the place has turned into a sort of half-kitsch, half-cool hipster hangout at weekends.

THE HILLS OF WEST JAVA

West Java, centered on the upland city of Bandung, is another country. By that I mean that as far as the Sundanese locals are concerned, it's not part of Java—that starts further east, at the linguistic and provincial frontier of the Citanduy River.

A High-Altitude Playground

The Dieng Plateau lies in the belly of an old volcano, 6,000 feet (1,800 meters) up in the very heart of Central Java. It has a collection of small but finely formed eighth-century temples, steaming volcanic vents and sulfur-tinted lakes, and great hiking. In the last few years it has turned into a major hotspot for the domestic backpacking crowd. At weekends dozens of young travelers from Yogyakarta, Semarang, and further afield turn up to climb the surrounding ridges, and there's a real buzz in the plateau's main village. It's a great place to come if you want to connect with this scene (there are several dozen homestays so you'll usually be able to find somewhere to stay, even at the busiest times), though if you'd prefer to enjoy a little more serenity, then all you need to do is visit midweek.

Java

100 km
50 miles

N

Sunda Kelapa
Fatahillah Square ★
★ *Lapangan Merdeka*
JAKARTA ■
Bogor ★ *Tangkuban Perahu*
Bogor's Botanic Gardens ★ *Puncak*
Bandung *J a v a*
Panaitan ★ *One-Palm Point*
Cirebon
Tegal *Pekalongan* *Semarang* *Kudus*
Karimunjawa Islands
Bawean
Gunung Muria 1602m
Jepara
Tuban
Suramadu *M a d u r a*
Ampel *Sumenep*
Gunung Penanggungan 1653m *Surabaya*
Citanduy River
Kawah Sikidang, Dieng Plateau
Gunung Merapi 2930m *Solo* *Candi Cetho*
Pangandaran *Borobudur* *Prambanan* *Candi Sukuh* *Gunung Lawu 3265m* *Madiun*
Cilacap *Gadjah Mada University* *Sosrowijayan* *Tawangmangu* *Ponorogo* *Gunung Kelud 1731m* *Trawas*
Batukaras *Yogyakarta* *Candi Ijo, Candi Banyunibo* *Candi Panataran* *Batu* *Gunung Bromo 2329m* *Tretes* *Malang* *Jember*
Pacitan *Blitar*
Kawah Ijen
B a l i
Banyuwangi
★ *G-Land*

Below Tea and tranquility: the uplands of Java are worlds apart from the busy cities, closer to sea level.

Left The beautiful botanic garden at Bogor was founded in 1817 by Caspar Reinwardt—the guy depicted on the monument here.

Above Batik is the most famous Javanese craft—not just a folksy thing for tourist souvenirs but a multi-million-dollar export industry.

The bits of West Java that get the most foreign visitors are Bogor—the old Dutch retreat that's these days pretty much a rainy suburb of Jakarta, though it still has a brilliant botanic garden—and Bandung, the provincial capital. Bandung is a very big city, but it's got a much cooler climate than Jakarta, and if you want to explore modern urban culture it's a great place, with a huge student population, and a reputation as a hothouse of rock and pop music. But my favorite bit of West Java is down on the coast around Pangandaran, a sleepy beach town (which is also the inspiration for "Halimunda" in Eka Kurniawan's magical-realist novels). Pangandaran itself is a good place to spend a few days, and a bit further west along the coast is the super-chilled surfers' village of Batu Karas.

ALONG THE NORTH COAST

Most travelers taking a jaunt through Java follow a southern route, through the mountains via Bandung and Yogyakarta. But if you stick to the north coast instead, and trace the main Jakarta-Surabaya highway and railway line, you'll have a chance to touch base in a string of cities that showcase the heritage of trade and immigration that have made Indonesia what it is. Start with the old royal town of Cirebon, then pass through the dusty batik-making center of Pekalongan to reach the Central Java capital at Semarang. This is a seriously big city—with all the good and bad that entails. But it's also got some of the finest Dutch-era architecture in Java, plus a huge ethnic-Chinese population, loads of incense-wreathed Chinese temples, and

some top-notch Chinese food. Beyond Semarang, my favorite corner of this north coast strip is the area around the outlying Gunung Muria volcano. This is a little world within a world, way off most tourist itineraries, and feeling somehow separate from the rest of Java. The main town is Kudus, which has a spectacular mosque which looks like a temple, and some distinctively Middle Eastern flavors in both its architecture and its cuisine. Sleepy Jepara, meanwhile, is the hopping-off point for trips to the beautiful Karimunjawa Islands.

THE JAVANESE HEARTLAND

The southern heartland of Central Java is the region that most travelers visit—and with good reason. There are the show-stopping Buddhist and Hindu temples at Borobudur and Prambanan, right up there with Angkor Wat and the Taj Mahal in the world wonder stakes. And then there's the grand old city of Yog-yakarta (the Ys are pronounced as Js, just so you know) which combines a regal pedigree with a bohemian vibe, and its estranged royal sibling, Solo, an hour up the road. Some travel snobs claim you should avoid Yogya and stick to Solo for a more "authentic" experience, but I reckon you should see both—Solo's definitely got a whiff of courtly dignity

that's missing in Yogya, but Yogya's got an arty, cosmopolitan, student-fueled vibe that's miss-ing in Solo. And what I love these days is that the traditional Yogyakarta budget travelers' quarter, Sosrowijayan, with its narrow alleys, homestays, and cafés, sees as many Indonesian backpackers as it does foreigners, which makes for some great cross-cultural interactions.

Above and left
In the heart of the Yogyakarta royal quarter, the Taman Sari water palace is a place of supernatural shenanigans, by some accounts.

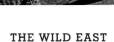

THE WILD EAST

For me, the huge mountain-studded province of East Java is where you'll find the real soul of the island—but I am probably a bit biased, having called the province home for a good few years. The provincial capital, Surabaya, is a seething, straight-speaking sort of city. It's got some wonderfully atmospheric neighborhoods in the historic districts near the port—especially the Arab quarter known as Ampel. But the real

Forgotten Javanese Temples

Everyone visits Borobudur and Prambanan, but there are plenty of temple-spotting alternatives without the crowds.

Candi Sukuh and Candi Cetho lie a few miles apart on the west-ern slopes of the Gunung Lawu volcano, close to the old royal city of Solo in Central Java. When it comes to location, these places are hard to beat, and the journey through the tea gar-dens to Candi Cetho in particular is stunning. Both temples date from the last decades of Hindu-Buddhism, and it seems like the craftsmen were indulging in a bit of end-of-days experimentation: some of the carvings are pretty much X-rated...

Further east, over the provincial border in East Java close to Blitar, you'll find Candi Panataran, a major temple complex in a lush setting of rice fields and palms. It might not match Borobudur when it comes to scale, but it has some similarly intricate bas-relief panels and the surrounding countryside is amongst the finest in Java.

Candi Cetho **(left)** and Candi Panataran **(below)** are well off the main tourist trail, and all the more atmospheric for it.

Left Not some desert waste in Central Asia, but the fantastical volcanic landscape around Bromo in East Java.

pleasures are out in the countryside beyond. The bits of East Java that most visitors see are the frenetically friendly little city of Malang, standing proud in a bowl of land between two mountain massifs; the much-photographed panorama at the Bromo-Tengger volcanic caldera; and the wonderful upland world of Kawah Ijen, with its coffee plantations, active volcanic crater, and famous sulfur miners—possibly Indonesia's toughest men.

But if at all possible you should get yourself a set of wheels and head out beyond these tick-box attractions. In the area around Trawas and Tretes, south of Surabaya, you'll find rice terrace landscapes which are more than a match for anything in Bali. Along the southern highway stretching from Ponorogo to Banyuwangi via Blitar and Jember you'll find epic roadside scenery and a string of small towns where you can check the pulse of Java (and get a tasty plate of nasi pecel while you're at it). And if you strike out down any of the lanes leading towards the coast, you'll probably find a sickle-shaped strip of sand under craggy limestone cliffs at journey's end.

The hardy sulfur miners of Kawah Ijen.

Holy Smoke!

If you want to come face to face with an active volcano without too much effort, then Java is the place to do it. There are sulfur-scented craters all the way along the island's mountain spine, and you can visit some of them without having to strap on your hiking boots. Gunung Bromo is one of Indonesia's "must-sees", and so long as it's not kicking off for a major eruption you can peer right down into the crater. For something a bit different, however, it's worth making the effort to get to Gunung Kelud, between Blitar and Malang. This is one of the most explosive of all Javanese mountains, but when it's behaving itself you can drive right into the crater via a tunnel. There used to be a huge, ominously smoking lava dome in the middle of the caldera, but it blew itself apart in an enormous explosion in 2014. Further west, Kawah Sikidang on the Dieng Plateau is an eerie volcanic wasteland with some furiously bubbling mud pools and sulfuric smoke seeping from the ground beneath your feet.

The Sleepy Island of Madura

The one thing that's not sleepy in Madura is the island's famous bull races.

Of all the islands in Indonesia, none has a worse reputation than Madura, a hundred-mile-long lozenge of land riding off the northeast coast of Java like a ship at anchor. It's said to be unbearably hot, unspeakably filthy, and populated entirely by foul-mouthed thugs—but all this comes entirely from Indonesians who've never actually been there and who base their ideas in popular prejudice against Madurese migrant workers. What you'll actually find if you cross Suramadu, the impressive suspension bridge which connects Madura to Surabaya, is a perfect off-the-beaten track adventure, with some very welcoming locals, and plenty of tasty sate to eat. The best place to base yourself is the eastern town of Sumenep, once a minor royal capital. It's a sleepy, easy-going community, with some fine old buildings, lots of beautiful countryside and some deserted beaches nearby.

THE ENDURING MAGIC OF BALI

Bali is a small island but, boy, does it loom large when it comes to the world's imaginings of Indonesia! It's fair to say that there's a whole lot of nonsense talked about Bali—whether by the hippy-dippy crew convinced that it's the most spiritual place on the planet, by the naysayers who make out that it's a tourism-destroyed hellhole, or even by the locals (who well understand the value of their island's image when it comes to business). But whatever anyone says: Bali really is special. It might be the genuinely distinctive Hindu-Balinese culture which sets the island a little apart from the rest of Indonesia. It might be the particularly gorgeous rice-fields-and-volcanoes landscapes. Or it might simply be a self-fulfilling prophecy—so many people for so many years have been focusing their travel fantasies on Bali that they willed a paradise into existence. In any case, I know I'll never get bored of Bali, and I know I'll never be one to say it's "too touristy"…

Like so many people, my own introduction to Indonesia came in the pocket of steamy, traffic-clogged mayhem that is southern Bali. Once upon a time the different communities here had clear green sawah between them, but these days the whole area is pretty much a single sprawling conurbation. The workaday Indonesian city of Denpasar lies at the center, shading off on either side into a hem of tourist areas.

The original Bali tourist town is Kuta, and this is the island at its maddest—a turbulent tangle of narrow streets, cheap hotels, and no-holds-barred nightlife, all fronting onto a wide beach. Depending on your point of view, Kuta is either the worst place in the world, or the ultimate beachside playground (it's worth remembering that loads of middle class Indonesians holiday here too, as well as the proverbial swarms of young Australian party animals). In the last few years I've been starting to feel like I might be getting a bit old for it myself, but it was where I took my first steps in Indonesia, so I'll always have a soft spot for Kuta.

To the north Kuta morphs via Legian into Seminyak. At first glance Seminyak looks little different from Kuta. The

Dinner with a sunset view at Jimbaran (**top**) and on the Bukit (**above**). It's easy to see why Bali is a popular honeymoon destination.

traffic's as bad, and it fronts onto the same super-long stretch of sand. But then you peer a bit closer and realize that the Gucci handbags here aren't cheap knock-offs; they're the real deal. Seminyak is where the Beautiful People—be they Jakarta supermodels or Hollywood royalty—hang out. As for me, I'm not a twenty-something hedonist any more, and I never quite made it into the ranks of the Beautiful People,

Every day is a festival day in Bali, with the calendar full of temple ceremonies.

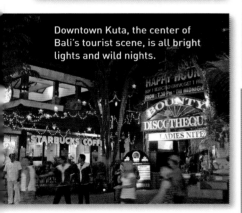

Downtown Kuta, the center of Bali's tourist scene, is all bright lights and wild nights.

so these days I usually head to the other side of southern Bali, and bed down in Sanur, a much sleepier sort of resort.

EAT, PRAY, LOVE

Imagine taking a pinch of Venice Beach and a smattering of San Francisco, adding a dollop of Byron Bay and a sprinkle of Dharamsala, throwing it all in the blender and serving it up as an organic smoothie with a palm leaf and a frangipani flower for a garnish. That's Ubud. This is where Elizabeth Gilbert came to find herself and find love, and though the place was already swarming with chakra-toting, art-buying, yoga-loving folks long before *Eat, Pray, Love*, these days the annual influx of wannabe Elizabeths has reached plague proportions.

Nusa Penida: Like Bali Thirty Years Ago

"Like Bali 30 years ago" is one of the most overused of all travel writing clichés. But here's the thing: there really is a place that's "like Bali 30 years ago", and believe it or not, it's actually part of Bali! Just an hour by boat from the busy beaches of Sanur—and almost within hailing distance of crowded holiday islet Nusa Lembongan—there's a craggy hulk of limestone by the name of Nusa Penida. This offshore fragment of Bali Province has been com-

pletely bypassed by the tourist boom of the past four decades. It's a place of potholed backroads and shady villages where a passing foreigner will still cause heads to turn, and at the bottom of looming cliffs there are bone-white beaches without a soul in sight. Change is going to come, though: they've already built the first upscale hotels, and plots of land in the northwest of the island are finally being snapped up by developers, so get there soon...

Bali in a Moment

First light on the ferry from Ketapang in Java to Gilimanuk at the western tip of Bali. A gang of carefree young English teachers—Aussies, Canadians, Brits—on one of our regular weekend excursions from Surabaya. An overnight train ride behind us, and a few hours on a bus ahead before we hit Kuta. Leaning bleary-eyed against the rail, watching the livid stain of the coming sunrise over the black hills of the West Bali National Park, and the excitement already building...

Kuta might be a manic resort these days, but it still has one of Bali's best beaches—and some of its finest sunsets.

The Gilis

They're not actually part of Bali, but these days the three specks of sandy soil known as "the Gilis" have become an essential appendage to the island for many visitors. The Gilis—Gili Trawangan, Gili Meno, and Gili Air—lie just off the northwest corner of Lombok, but most visitors blaze directly across the strait from Bali by speedboat without ever setting foot on Lombok proper. There's no doubt that the Gilis are beautiful—spots of low-lying land ringed with blinding white beaches and still totally free of motor-

ized traffic. But the biggest, most popular island, Gili Trawangan, is a bit of a zoo these days, taking its style key from Thailand's busiest tourist islands. If that sort of thing appeals, then you'll love it; if it doesn't, then head elsewhere. Also, be aware that there have been rumbles of local discontent with the low-spend, high-alcohol element of the tourist trade in recent years, and talk of trying to nudge things in the

direction of smaller numbers, bigger wallets, and better behavior. Foreign-owned backpacker hostels with pile-'em-high dorms recently fell foul of a local bylaw restricting the number of guests allowed to stay in one room, and there are rumors that Gili T's days as a party island might be numbered.

But don't get me wrong—I still love Ubud, even though the traffic on the main streets is increasingly apocalyptic, and the backroads that fronted onto rice fields the day before yesterday are now lined with cafés and galleries. Ubud is one place where the locals have managed to hold onto ownership of a lot of the tourist industry, which—along with the fact that a lot of Jakarta hipsters now holiday here too—does something to assuage the idea of a sort of New Age hippie-colonialism!

ON THE ROAD IN BALI

There's a whole lot more to Bali than Ubud and the south. Lower-key resorts, each with its own distinct vibe, are scattered around the island—from the diving scene on the offshore island of Nusa Lembongan, to the lazy beach town of Lovina up on the north coast. And every few years a spot that was

ticking along just under the tourist radar for decades suddenly gets "discovered" and goes big. The latest places to get that treatment are Amed up at the far northwest corner of Bali, which used to be just a handful of very low key dive resorts on a craggy strip of coast, but which is now *the* place for both middle-aged divers and twenty-

something backpackers, and Munduk up in the mountains. And then there's my personal favorite Bali hideaway, the Sidemen Valley, which stretches north from Klunkung towards the mighty Gunung Agung volcano. It'll probably be swamped with boutique villas within a couple of years, but it'll still have one of the finest natural settings in Bali.

Bali off the Beaten Track

Since the very first foreign holidaymaker set foot in Bali people have been moaning and groaning and claiming the place has been ruined by tourism. But those grumblers don't have imagination or a motorbike. You really need to get your own set of wheels to access it, but "the real Bali" is very much alive and kicking. Drive out along the quiet highway from Amlapura to Rendang in eastern Bali, then swing up any of the lanes running north towards Gunung Agung; head north out of Tabanan towards Gunung Batukaru then swing right or left down whichever side road takes your fancy; keep rocking on the rolling coast road beyond the easternmost hotel in Amed; heck, take two steps sideways off any main road anywhere in Bali,

and you'll be into a world of quiet village rhythms that time-travelers from the 1930s might still recognize. And as soon as Amed, Munduk, Sidemen and all the other current "see it now before it's spoilt" spots are overwhelmed, you can guarantee there'll be another mountain hamlet or tucked-away beach community waiting in the wings. There's still plenty of Bali to go round.

The mountains and the sea: Amed's superb bay with Mt Agung in the background.

The water palace at Tirtagangga is one of the many treasures you might stumble upon during a Bali road trip.

Above, top and right Bali
effortlessly combines its role
as the ultimate playground for
Indonesia and the world—surf,
parties, all-round fun—with a
deep commitment to its own
cultural and religious
traditions, most obvious in the
thousands of active temples.

Padangbai (East Bali)

Flavor-of-the-month destinations in Bali can morph at lighting
speed. You visit one year and discover a handful of guesthouses
and the first hint of a buzz, then come back 18 months later and
find a rash of villas, restaurants and travel agencies. But there's
one place that's somehow kept its original atmosphere, and
that's the sleepy harbor community of Padangbai, where the
ferries and speedboats depart for Lombok. A few years back it
looked like it was on the brink of a boom, and an abortive resort
development made a mess of the hillside behind the gorgeous
little Bias Tugel beach. But then, somehow, the pace slowed
again and Padangbai slipped back into its old-school tropical
torpor. It's a great place to chill out for a few days, and there's a
real village atmosphere in the alleys back from the seafront.

The Dark Side of Paradise?

While the Eat, Pray, Love crowd still like to
patronizingly proclaim Bali the ultimate tropical
paradise, peopled entirely by sensitive, spiritual,
artistic souls, they have a counterpoint in the
excitable Australian journalists and embittered
expats who clog up the Internet telling tales
of the island as a sort of modern-day Sodom
and Gomorrah, awash with drugs, crime, and
violence.

There's absolutely no question that the
seething southern areas of Bali have their fair
share of darkness. Petty—and sometimes more
serious—crime is a significant issue; there's a
busy and chaotic drugs trade (which you'd be an
idiot of the first rank to go anywhere near); the
Kuta nightlife scene has a shady undercurrent of
organized crime; and there's plenty of Wild West-
style double-crossing when it comes to business
deals and land sales (in which foreigners can
sometimes be the perpetrators as well as the
victims). But all this stuff is par for the course in
overdeveloped tourist areas the world over, from
Ko Samui to the Costa del Sol.

Here's my theory: the negative hyperbole you
sometimes hear about Bali is directly related
to the similarly hyperbolic positive fluff. People
are so primed with legends of the island as the
ultimate tropical paradise, that the moment they
lose their wallet to a pickpocket or get stung for a
bribe by a bent traffic cop they tumble into disil-
lusioned bitterness. The truth is that Bali is just
a place, like any other, with good people and bad
people, good deeds and bad deeds. It was never
really a paradisiacal otherworld (it has a notably
violent history, and until the birth of the tourist
trade in the early 20th century outside opinions
of Bali and the Balinese tended to be pretty negative). But if you keep a sense of perspective, hold
onto your wallet, never buy drugs—and think
long and hard before succumbing to the dream of
expat life in a Canggu villa—then it's still one of
the coolest places on the planet to visit.

SUPERSIZED SUMATRA

The first thing to say about Sumatra is that it's big—and I mean really big. The trouble with traveling in an archipelagic nation is that you get used to looking at the map of one island, and sometimes forget to readjust your sense of scale when you move onto the next place. I'm most used to looking at the map of Java, so in Bali I'm forever catching myself out when what I'd subconsciously assumed would be a half-day journey takes only an hour; and in Sumatra I'm always struggling to work out why a destination I'd figured on reaching by teatime is still miles away two days later!

As well as being bigger than many countries in mainland Southeast Asia, Sumatra is also strikingly empty. If you've been in busy Java or Bali beforehand you'll find yourself peering out of the bus window as you wind your way along the meandering highways, and wondering where all the people have gone. From the rugged spine of the Bukit Barisan, the thickly forested mountain range that runs down the entire western seaboard of the island, to the deep, swampy levels of the eastern lowlands, the gaps between the urban centers are big here. Little surprise, then, that this is the one part of Indonesia where there are still a few tigers on the prowl…

THE NORTHERN CIRCUIT
Compared to the smaller islands to the south, Sumatra gets only a trickle of travelers, and almost all those who do make it to Sumatra stick to a tight little circuit. They touch down in Medan, which isn't an easy city to love (though it's well worth checking out the beautiful Tjong A Fie Mansion in the old Chinese quarter—a rare example of properly preserved Indonesia

urban heritage), then hightail it for the steamy green village of Bukit Lawang on the edge of the Gunung Leuser National Park—the best place to meet orangutans in Indonesia. After that it's a quick about-turn southwards to Danau Toba, possibly with a stop-off in Berastagi on the way. Then it's back to Medan…

These places are all definitely major highlights, and well worth seeing, but if you want to properly get into the guts

Travel in Sumatra can be tough going, but that just means you'll appreciate a relaxing paradise like Danau Toba **(top and above)** all the more when you get there!

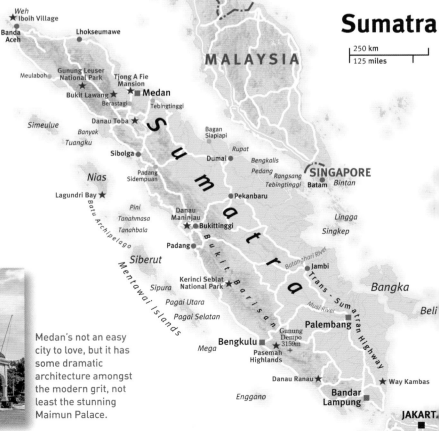

Sumatra

250 km
125 miles

Medan's not an easy city to love, but it has some dramatic architecture amongst the modern grit, not least the stunning Maimun Palace.

Above right There's no doubt about which species gets star billing in the Sumatran jungle. The island is one of only two places on earth (the other is Borneo) where you'll find wild orangutans.

of Sumatra you might want to head a bit further afield—up north into Aceh, which has turned into a proper new travel frontier since the decades-long conflicted between separatists and the state ended in the aftermath of the 2004 tsunami, or down south into the untrammeled nether regions of the island.

ON THE EQUATOR

The equator spans the midriff of Sumatra like a belt. Not far below it, on the west coast, is the city of Padang, home of the magnificent cuisine that tops the list of all Indonesia's regional cooking styles. A disproportionate number of the foreign travelers who pass through the airport here come dragging padded surfboard bags. They're all bound for

Sumatra in a Moment

A chilly dawn on the high slopes of Gunung Dempo, the vast volcano that towers over the Pasemah Highlands. Shivering in the shelter of the lichen-bearded trees beneath the summit. Watching the glowing blanket of cloud slowly pulling back and finding all Sumatra at our feet: the dark spine of the Bukit Barisan stretching away north and south; the tea gardens taking on a dull shine in the yellow east; and to the west, beyond a knot of ragged ridges and ten thousand feet (3,000 meters) below, the powder-blue smudge of the Indian Ocean...

the offshore Mentawai Islands, for which Padang is the gateway. Most non-surfers, however, head inland, up into the craggy green heartlands of the Minangkabau people around Bukittinggi. In this region you'll find some classic volcanoes to climb, and a sort of miniature, less-visited version of Danau Toba, the equally beautiful Danau Maninjau—plus loads of awesome Padang-style food, of course.

Sumatra's wildest architecture is found in the Minangkabau regions. Some say the dramatic roof-lines of these *rumah gadang* represent the horns of a buffalo.

Tiger! Tiger!

Everyone who goes to Bukit Lawang gets to meet orangutans, but there's another jungle resident that still—just about—maintains a ghostly presence in Sumatra. Your chances of actually seeing a tiger, however, are slim to none. There are probably fewer than 500 of them left in the whole of Sumatra, and though there are a good few in the Gunung Leuser National Park you categorically won't see any prowling around Bukit Lawang. Real tiger territory is to the north, on the Aceh side of the park, but you could trek here for months and count yourself lucky if you saw so much as a single paw-print. The other tiger hotspot is the vast, mountainous Kerinci Seblat National Park, but this is a place with next to no tourist infrastructure. The only Sumatran national park with a proper set-up for visitors (other than the little Bukit Lawang pocket of Gunung Leuser) is Way Kambas, down south in Lampung, and not too far from Jakarta. It has eco-lodges, elephant rides, the whole she-bang—and also a tiny handful of tigers. Hardly anyone ever spots them though, but you will almost certainly see one of the biggest herds of wild elephants in Indonesia, which is some consolation!

Islands in the Stream

Look at the map. Strung down the western side of Sumatra, a hundred miles (161 kilometers) off shore, is a long, long chain of islands. Some are mere specks, halfway to nothing in the great blue blank of the Indian Ocean. But others are rough oblongs of limestone as big as Bali. They begin with Pulau Simeulue in the north, and follow an arrow-straight angle southwards through the little cluster of the Banyak Islands; past Nias' foreboding hulk; the Batu Archipelago; then the long line of the Mentawais, before the chain breaks, leaving a vast reach of empty ocean—marked only by a miniscule pinprick called Pulau Mega, small beyond maps even. The final, southernmost speck is Pulau Enggano, which takes its name from the Portuguese word for "mistake". No one knows how or when it got that moniker, but it certainly conjures a bleak image of some ragged, salt-scarred crew in a worm-addled car-rack meeting bitter disappointment on a stony shoreline.

Anyone with an ounce of wanderlust in their soul only needs to glance at this chain of islands on the charts to start dreaming of fabulous journeys—but for many years the going has been tough hereabouts. Isolated in stormy seas, swathed with sticky jungle, swarming with malarial mosquitoes, and home to some decidedly warlike tribal cultures, the islands managed to remain aloof from the influences of all of the major world religions that spread through Indonesia until the twentieth century. They also kept the Dutch colonialists very much at bay.

For a long time the only part of the chain that saw significant visitor action was Nias, the biggest island of the lot, usually reached from the mainland port of Sibolga southwest of Lake Toba. It's always been a peculiar sort of place: beloved of anthropologists and home to a remarkable traditional

culture of high-roofed villages and megaliths, albeit one heavily overlaid with Christianity, but with a not entirely undeserved reputation for being one of the very few places in Indonesia that isn't instantly and overwhelmingly welcoming. As for the rest of the islands—they were about as far off the beaten track as you could possibly get.

But surfing changed all that. Nias' Lagundri Bay was the starting point, but the minute surfers started looking at the shipping charts they realized that there would be world-class waves breaking along the shores of just about every island in the chain. A few hardy adventurers and a few well-funded international pros on chartered yachts came first, then a high-end surf charter industry developed, followed by a scattering of camps onshore in the Mentawai Islands. The surf network continues to spread, and that's made it easier for non-wave-riding travelers to visit too. Mentawai has some of the wildest jungle trekking in Indonesia.

Above and left Perfect, uncrowded surf, picture-perfect islets, and strong traditional cultures: the Mentawai islands have a lot to offer.

The Trans-Sumatran Highway

It's one hell of a road. If you knuckle down for the hard slog of overland travel in Sumatra, you will find yourself spending many hours on its meandering ribbon of cracked gray asphalt: the Trans-Sumatran High-way, stretching 1,500 miles (2,400 kilometers) all the way from Banda Aceh in the north to Bandar Lampung in the south. Around the big cities and the more densely populated areas it is a solid freeway, with multiple lanes in places. But while a planned upgrade of its entire length is underway, there are still many, many miles where it's nothing more than a country road through the forest, and during the rainy season it is often blocked by landslides and fallen trees. Mind you, even that's an improvement—a couple of decades back, in many of these sections it was still a dirt track.

Indiana Jones Land

An open boat putters along a coffee-colored river under a blank white sky. Tall stands of reeds run down to the water's edge, and beyond them the forest rises in a knotty wall of branches and creepers. You can hear the sound of the insects above the rattle of the outboard motor. The only sign of human life is an occasional glimpse of a ramshackle wooden hut—built on tall stilts with good reason, for tigers still come creeping out of the forest here from time to time. The world feels a long way away, but within those tangles of trees and undergrowth there are great moldering mounds of red brick, crumbling pavilions, and the traces of grand buildings. It is the ruins of a lost civilization...

The small city of Jambi, deep in the swampy lowlands of eastern Sumatra is a million miles from most tourist itineraries. This is a region where Indonesia begins to fray into deltas and muddy

islets, the land giving way uneasily to the shallows of the Melaka Strait, one of the world's greatest maritime thoroughfares since the dawn of history. The city is a friendly place, but the only real reason to come here is to take that boat ride, 15 miles (24 kilometers) downstream along the Batang Hari River to Muara Jambi. A thousand years ago this was the seat of the mighty trading state of Malayu, and its temple ruins still dot the forest. Made of brick rather than limestone, they can hardly match the deeply decorated glories of Java; just a few of the central temples have been cleared and restored, while most still lie in ruins. But you'll generally have the place entirely to yourself, and as you wander out along the forest trails beyond the central complex you can easily let yourself pretend to be an adventurous pioneer, exploring some utterly forgotten world in search of archeological treasure—which is not something you could very easily do amongst the hordes of sightseers at Borobudur!

THE DEEP SOUTH

No one goes to the southernmost provinces of Sumatra—Lampung, Bengkulu, and South Sumatra. A few years back I spent a month wandering around this neck of the woods, and I didn't meet a single other foreigner the whole time. What I did find, though, were places that would be crawling with travelers if they were in Thailand or Vietnam, or in Java for that matter—all of which goes to show what a fickle thing tourism is. If you want a proper off-the-beaten track adventure, for my money this is one of the best corners of Indonesia to choose. My highlights hereabouts include Bengkulu City, surely one of the sleepiest, loneliest of provincial capitals, and formerly one of the sleepiest, loneliest outposts of the British Empire, still studded with colonial relics. The silvery sheet of Danau Ranau, straddling the Lampung-South Sumatra border and hemmed by sheer mountainsides and forests where there are still a few tigers, is like Toba without the tourists. And the quiet cool of the Pasemah Highlands is a place to stretch your legs and strike out for volcanic summits.

Above Huge, rubbery and smelling of rotting flesh, the giant Rafflesia flower is one of the strangest things in the Sumatran forest.

Your chances of encountering a super-rare Sumatran rhino **(above)** in the wild are slim, but you can get up close with an elephant at Tangkahan in the Gunung Leuser National Park **(left)**.

THE OUTER ISLANDS: WHERE THINGS GET REALLY WEIRD AND WILD

Java, Bali, and Sumatra are just three of Indonesia's 17,000-odd islands. Beyond their shores the archipelago sweeps onwards, across far horizons, all the way to the edge of the Pacific Ocean. There's much, much more out there than even the most tireless traveler could ever see in a single lifetime—a fact that thrills me and frustrates me in equal measure!

Above Here be dragons: the craggy, sun-scorched landscapes of Komodo are like a real-life Jurassic Park...

It's in the remoter reaches of Nusa Tenggara, Maluku, Papua, Sulawesi, and Kalimantan that the Indonesia of shopping malls and smartphones seems most distant. And it's out here that you'll encounter the roughest of the rough aspects of Indonesian travel—the most torturous transport, the grimiest accommodation, and the most gruesome food. But that's all more than worthwhile when you find yourself standing in the middle of a village of towering thatched houses in an amphitheater of green mountains, or tentatively laying a first footprint into the powdery sand of a virgin beach that's as far from Kuta as you could possibly imagine.

EAST OF BALI

Nusa Tenggara is my favorite venue for island-hopping in all Indonesia. The "Islands of the Southeast" are the string of stepping-stones stretching between Bali and Timor. Each landfall here opens a totally new view. The journeys between individual islands are often short, but each is utterly distinctive in landscape, culture, religion, and even ethnicity. And while there are a couple of hotspots that get thousands of visitors, most of Nusa Tenggara is miles away from well-trodden trails. As you head eastwards the outlines of pre-Islamic and pre-Christian traditions start to show through the surface, and when you finally reach the end of the road at the furthest extremity of Flores, and step from a rattletrap bus onto a rickety ferry, there's a sense of stepping off the map, and out of the 21st century.

ISLAND BY ISLAND

Lombok is the first landfall, heading east into Nusa Tenggara. Its trio of off-shore sand-spots, the Gilis, get hordes of visitors, and there are a couple of low-key resorts elsewhere—at Senggigi and Kuta (not to be confused with its Bali namesake). The south coast has some great surf, but for me Lombok is all about the 12,000-foot (3,700-meter) hulk that rises from its heart. This is Rinjani, the second highest volcano in Indonesia (Kerinci in Sumatra, 260 feet [80 meters] taller, takes the top spot). Rinjani is one of the best trek-king destinations in the country—usually tackled as a three-day traverse, up to the summit and around the caldera rim. But it's also the linchpin of a glori-ous surrounding landscape, and—especially around Bayan and Senaru—some intriguing cultural traditions.

Heading on beyond Lombok you reach Sumbawa. It's a peculiar place—just as beautiful as its neighbors, but noticeably poorer than either Lombok or Flores. Some people claim that it never really recovered from the mas-sive Tambora volcanic eruption in

Nusa Tenggara in a Moment

On a rusting ferry, lumbering east from Larantuka through the night. Sleeping under a thin blanket on the deck and waking in a gray dawn with volcanoes smoking to the south and outriggers creeping offshore from lost villages in the lontar palms of Pantar. And then, with the light brightening and the swell surging creamy over the rocks at the head of Kalabahi Bay, hearing a shout of "Ikan paus!" and turning in time to see the great gray back of a whale arching to starboard...

Above Sumba locals watch the unfolding spectacle of the Pasola— a hell-for-leather ritual battle on horseback.

1815. Most visitors who actually hang around in Sumbawa are there for the surf—either around Maluk in the west, or around Hu'u in the east—but there's plenty of adventure waiting in the hills if you really want to get off the radar.

After Lombok, the island that gets most visitors is Flores, a snaking tranche of territory where barnlike Catholic churches stand beneath misty mountain ridges, and where local smiles are colored red with betel nut. Most of those visitors fly into the westernmost port of Labuanbajo then head off to explore the dragon-haunted islets and coral gardens of the Komodo National Park. The first time I went to Labuanbajo it felt like a harbor at the ends of the earth; these days it's got flashy Italian restaurants. But as soon as you head east into the hills wild Flores takes over again, with dizzying mountain roads and fine traditional villages.

South of the main chain you'll find Timor—the western half of which still belongs to Indonesia. This is where Kupang, the only proper city in the region, is to be found. It's a slow-paced sort of place, with a easygoing charm and some very interesting characters hanging around the waterfront bars—plus the most insanely decorated bemo (public minibuses) in Indonesia. Inland, meanwhile, there are scrubby hills, studded with villages.

The final big Nusa Tenggara island is Sumba, which is my hands-down favorite place for coming face-to-face with "traditional culture" in Indonesia —think wild grasslands looking more like the Serengeti than Southeast Asia,

Above In the misty uplands of western Flores, the traditional villages—like this one at Wae Rebo—look like something out of a fantasy movie.

high-roofed village houses huddling together like witches' covens, and a powerful current of ancestor-veneration, just beneath the Christian surface. The western township of Waikabubak is the best starting point for adventures here.

The five big islands of Nusa Tenggara are only the start. There are plenty of other places, each with distinct cultures and languages of their own. Alor, at the very easternmost extreme of the chain, gets a bit of low-key diver traffic these days, via twin-prop flights from Kupang, but hardly anyone bothers to explore its traditional villages where

Nusa Tenggara

Kangean

Tengah Islands

Jampea

Bonerate

250 km
125 miles

N

Gili Islands

Gunung Rinjani 3726m

Moyo I.

Gunung Tambora 2851m

Dompu

Bima

Komodo National Park

Labuanbajo

Ruteng

Flores

Maumere

Lembata

Pantar

Alor

Lombok

Mataram

Sumbawa

Pantai Merah

Bajawa

Ende

Kelimutu

TIMOR LESTE

Desert Point

Lakey Peak Fu'u

Wae Rebo

Bena

Nusa   Tenggara

Kampung Tarung

Waikabubak

Waingapu

Timor

Sumba

Soe

Boti

Oehala Waterfall

Kupang

Sabu

Rote

Nembrala

Tana Toraja stands out even among Indonesia's wealth of destinations, with its unearthly traditional architecture **(above left)**, bloody funerary sacrifices **(above)** and eye-catching tau-tau grave markers **(left)**.

of the village mosques. As a whole, Sulawesi lies well off the main travelers' pathways through Indonesia, but within its strange parameters there are individual destinations that rank high up on the national list of must-sees.

The premier Sulawesi travel venue, up in the highlands of the island's southwest leg, is Tana Toraja. This is one of my top places to visit in the whole country, packing a killer combo of green-drenched natural glory, rice terrace panoramas, the most dramatic village architecture in the country, and a traditional culture that's forging successfully ahead in the modern world. What else could you ask for?

Although it's Sulawesi's main tourist destination, the fact that it still takes some getting to—usually a domestic flight from Bali or Java to Makassar, then a ten-hour bus ride up into the hills—means that Toraja is still far from being swamped by visitors, even at the busiest times. But if you do want to dodge whatever meager crowds there are, then Toraja has a less trammeled sibling, west over the ridges in Mamasa, where they have their own brand of boat-roofed traditional houses, and their own green mountain scenery. Heading north from Toraja along a developing travelers' trail, you'll reach Tentena on the shores of lovely Lake Poso. It's a great place to rest up after bone-rattling bus rides, with freshwater beaches, waterfalls, and ancient burial caves in the countryside nearby.

you'll hear stories of spirit-dragons and other strange things if you ask the right questions. Between Alor and Flores, meanwhile, there are even smaller landfalls—Pantar, Adonara, Lembata, and Solor—which get very, very few visitors, but all of which have mountains to climb, empty beaches, and strong traditional cultures to investigate.

SPIDERY SULAWESI

On the map Sulawesi looks like a quadruple-limbed monster, flailing wildly in the middle of Indonesia. On the ground, meanwhile, it's a place of endless interlocked ridges, rising into knotty green ranges from cobalt-blue shorelines where the light shines back in bright stars from the steel domes

Further north lies Teluk Tomini, Sulawesi's great central bay. Set in its blue heart are the Togeans, a clutch of craggy islands, thickly forested, fringed with coral, and with a handful of stilt-built fishing villages and a scattering of dive resorts and easy-going beachside backpacker hangouts.

Finally, at the northernmost tip of the island, is Manado. Nearby there's top-class diving at Bunaken, weird things to eat in the inland villages, and monkey-haunted jungles to explore.

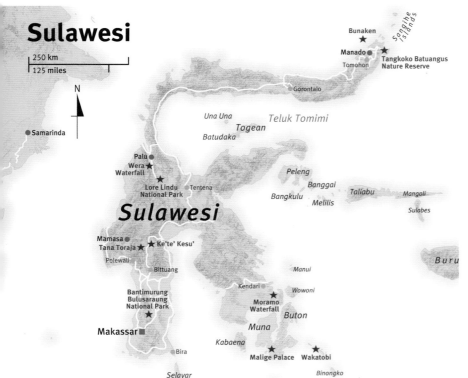

Sulawesi

250 km
125 miles

N

Samarinda

Bunaken ★
Sangihe Islands
Manado ●
Tomohon ● Tangkoko Batuangus Nature Reserve

Gorontalo

Una Una
Togean
Teluk Tomini
Batudaka

Palu ●
Wera ★
Waterfall
Lore Lindu National Park ● Tentena

Peleng
Banggai
Bangkulu
Melilis
Taliabu
Mangoli
Sulabes

Sulawesi

Mamasa ●
Tana Toraja ★ ★ Ke'te' Kesu'
Polewali

Bittuang

Manui
Kendari
Wowoni

Bantimurung Bulusaraung National Park ★

Moramo Waterfall
Buton
Muna

Makassar ■

Kabaena

Bira

Malige Palace ★ Wakatobi ★

Selayar

Binongko

Buru

The traditional—and decidedly cheeky—nickname for these proboscis monkeys in Kalimantan is Orang Belanda, which means "Dutchman"!

Kalimantan

INTO THE GREEN: KALIMANTAN

Borneo. It's one of those place names that does strange things to anyone with even the mildest case of wanderlust. They get a faraway look in their eyes, and you can tell that their mind has left the room and is paddling up a coffee-colored jungle river, or wandering somewhere beneath vast canopies of cloud forest. Then they come back to earth and explain that they're not actually sure where Borneo is…

To clear things up, Borneo is that massive blot of an island north of Java. It's split between three countries, with Malaysia and tiny Brunei taking the top tranche, and Indonesia occupying the bottom three-quarters, a region known as Kalimantan. The swampy, river mouth fringes of Kalimantan (don't come expecting pretty beaches hereabouts) have been the setting for small estuary kingdoms for hundreds of years, dominated by local Malay people, but with Chinese, Arab, and other settlers added to the mix. Inland, meanwhile, long, snaking rivers reach deep into jungle country, the territory of the Dayak peoples who've called Borneo home for longer than anyone else.

These days you shouldn't come to Kalimantan expecting to step straight into a Joseph Conrad novel. The old estuary sultanates have mostly turned into busy, gritty river cities—some with a certain dash of oil-money-fueled swagger; others tattered outposts of mud and traffic—while big swaths of one-time jungle have been logged out and turned over to palm oil plantations or mining. But if you roll up your sleeves and plunge in, there's still loads of magic in the green heart of Kalimantan.

Above Banjarmasin is sometimes called "The Venice of the East". That's stretching things a bit, but the floating market is certainly colorful.

Left The indigenous Dayaks of Kalimantan have a powerful sense of identity, celebrated here in traditional dance.

Below In places like Tanjung Puting, the rivers still serve as major roads connecting the interior to the coast.

The place that generates the most excitement has got to be the Tanjung Puting National Park, on the coast of Central Kalimantan. If you're after a budget orangutan encounter with a banana pancakes backpacker scene attached, then you're much better off heading to Bukit Lawang in Sumatra.

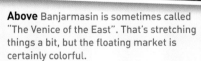

But if you want to pay a bit more, and get to meet the gingery primates by way of an atmospheric riverboat journey into proper wilderness, then this is definitely the place to come. Elsewhere, the mighty Mahakam River stretches from the sea at Samarinda way back into the very center of the island, and is open for river journeys deep into the interior. Amongst the other Kalimantan hotspots are trekking opportunities in the hilly Dayak country around Loksado in South Kalimantan, and the coral gardens of the Derawan Archipelago off the eastern coast.

INFINITY ISLANDS: MALUKU

It's as if they took all the bits that wouldn't fit in anywhere else, and made them into Maluku. Sprawling across the huge gap between Sulawesi, Papua, and Nusa Tenggara, Maluku is made up of more than a thousand individual islands—from Halmahera in the north (which looks eerily like Sulawesi's miniature twin) to the scattered outposts of Tanimbar in the south. This is where the idea that Indonesia is the world's largest archipelagic state really hits home; a limitless scattering of deep green jewels, each with a gilding of pale sand, flung at all angles on a setting of the brightest blue. You could spend a whole lifetime here, zigzagging back and forth across the Banda and Seram seas and never run out of fresh landfalls.

Needless to say, the going is often slow in Maluku. Ambon and Ternate are what pass for cities in this part of the world, and that's where you'll touch down when you come in by air from Sulawesi or Java. Beyond that you're into the realm of fragile propeller aircraft and lumbering ferries.

The place in Maluku that really sets travelers' hearts aflutter is a cluster of tiny islets so small that they barely feature on the map. Today the ten tiny pinpricks of volcanic earth that make up the Banda Archipelago are suffused with soporific stillness, all drooping palms, shimmering seas, and a few mildewed fortifications and rusting cannons to hint that something important happened here once upon a time. Visitors come, scrambling for the tenuous air and sea connections from Ambon, to enjoy all that, as well as the magnificent undersea attractions. But in the past foreigners set their sights on Banda with more rapacious intent. This was once the true center of "the Spice Islands", the world's only source of nutmeg. In fact, Banda was ultimately the spicy kernel from which the entire European empire in Indonesia sprouted, which in turn eventually became the independent republic of the present day.

Banda is not all there is in Maluku, though; far from it. The Kei Archipelago comes snapping at Banda's heels in the ultimate island paradise stakes; the dark interiors of Seram and Halmahera have potential for pioneering treks; and way, way down south the isolated landfalls of Southeast Maluku—from Wetar to Tanimbar—make for real castaway territory.

Above What lies beneath? The waters off Ternate are so clear that you don't even need a snorkel to see what's going on.

Nutmeg **(left)** was once worth more than its weight in gold. Little wonder that it prompted the Dutch traders who built Fort Belgica on Bandaniera **(top left)** to sail halfway round the world.

TO THE FRONTIER: PAPUA

Every country has one: a region that's somehow outside the pale of the national "mainstream". And Indonesia being a very big place, its own national outland is flat-out enormous—fully half of the second biggest island on earth.

Papua—the Indonesian-governed western chunk of New Guinea— has always dangled at the end of tenuous connections with the rest of the country. Its cultures and ethnicities have always stood apart, even in the stupendous diversity of Indonesia. The Dutch colonialists only took their first steps here very late in the imperial day, and then held onto the place for a decade and a half after the rest of Indonesia gained its independence. For most Indonesians today Papua is an exotic, "othered" place, either a romantic frontier for exploration and missionary activity, or the butt of a bad joke, peopled by ungrateful primitives. For those looking back in the other direction, meanwhile, Indonesia tends to seem like an unwelcome and oppressive colonial interloper. Not the happiest corner of the archipelago, then, but for travelers there's always an irresistible appeal in a place with a "frontier" quality.

The bits of Papua that get the most visitors are the area off the western tip of the Bird's Head Peninsula, and the

Above Putting on a show: Asmat villagers in southern Papua demonstrate their traditional canoeing techniques.

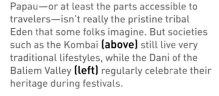

lost world of Baliem in the territory's mountain core. Sorong, the westernmost town in Papua, is the hopping-off point for the crystal waters of Raja Ampat, dive destination par excellence. Baliem, meanwhile, was going merrily about its business of rearing pigs and growing sweet potato without the outside world even knowing it existed until 1938,

when an American explorer overflying the wild green interior of Papua looked out of the window of his light aircraft, saw a huge, mountain-ringed valley scattered with villages and terraced fields, and wondered if he was hallucinating. These days planes are still the only way in, via the provincial capital at Jayapura, and the valley gets marketed as a sort

Papau—or at least the parts accessible to travelers—isn't really the pristine tribal Eden that some folks imagine. But societies such as the Kombai **(above)** still live very traditional lifestyles, while the Dani of the Baliem Valley **(left)** regularly celebrate their heritage during festivals.

of "Stone Age" trekking destination, which is more than a little insulting to the locals. Mind you, a fair few of them make a decent living as tour guides, so they probably don't mind!

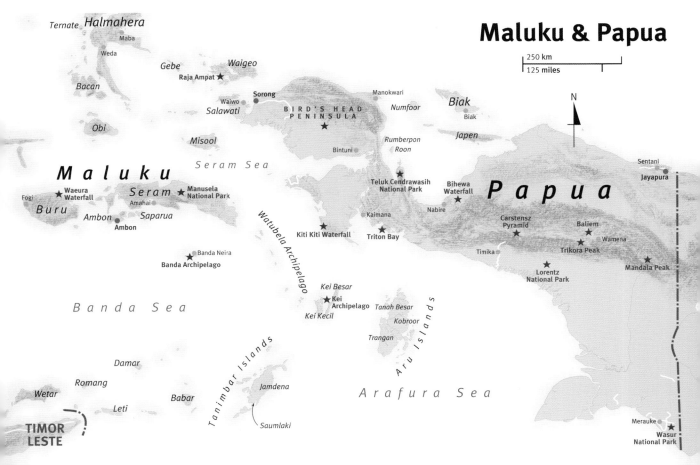

Maluku & Papua

250 km
125 miles

N

Ternate *Halmahera*
Maba
Weda
Gebe *Waigeo*
Bacan Raja Ampat ★
Waiwo Sorong Manokwari
Obi *Salawati* BIRD'S HEAD Numfoor *Biak*
PENINSULA Biak
Misool Bintuni Rumberpon *Japen*
Seram Sea Roon
Sentani
M a l u k u Teluk Cendrawasih Bihewa Jayapura
National Park Waterfall
Seram ★ Manusela *P a p u a*
Fogi ★ Waeura National Park Kaimana Nabire
Waterfall Amahai Carstensz
Buru Saparua Pyramid *Baliem*
Ambon Timika Wamena
Ambon ★ Banda Neira Kiti Kiti Waterfall ★ Trikora Peak
Banda Archipelago ★ Triton Bay Mandala Peak
Lorentz
Watubela Archipelago National Park
B a n d a S e a *Kei Besar*
★ *Kei*
Archipelago *Tanah Besar*
Kei Kecil Kobroor
Trangan
Damar *Jamdena* *A r a f u r a S e a*
Romang
Wetar Leti *Babar* *Saumlaki*
Merauke
**TIMOR
LESTE** *Tanimbar Islands* *Aru Islands* ★ Wasur
National Park

TRAVELING IN INDONESIA: SOME ESSENTIAL TRAVEL TIPS

With any luck, this book will have convinced you that you need to visit Indonesia—that is if you're not already out there, somewhere on the road with a mouthful of rendang and an earful of Marjinal. But when it comes to a country this big—and with so many watery bits between the landmasses—it can be hard to know where to start when it comes to making travel plans. With that in mind, we'll wrap up this journey through Indonesia in book form with a few practical pointers to get you going on your journey through the country on the ground.

Times have changed. Indonesia has been a legendary travel destination since the days of the overland Hippie Trail through Asia, but back then the going was seriously tough for any backpacker on a budget. You launched yourself into the archipelago by boat from Singapore or Malaysia, hoping eventually to make it to Bali though with little clue how long it would take to get there. Even when I first arrived at the dawn of the 21st century long-haul ferry rides and grim ordeals in wrecked buses were often the order of the day—and as for finding an Internet connection in the outer islands? Forget it…

But now, there's a surging economy, a burgeoning budget airline network, and a sophisticated local traveler community—and Wi-Fi just about everywhere.

GETTING TO INDONESIA

The great game-changer of the last few decades when it comes to Indonesian travel has been the rise of budget air travel—both within and without the country. Jakarta and Bali are still the only obvious points of arrival for long-haulers (there are virtually no flights to destinations outside Asia from anywhere else, bar a couple of links to Australia from Nusa Tenggara). But if you're coming in from a neighboring country, the competing flock of low-cost carriers opens up all sorts of other possibilities.

There are budget flights from Singapore and Kuala Lumpur to virtually every city with an airport in Sumatra and Java, plus a handful of destinations in Kalimantan and Sulawesi. There are also a good number of budget connections from Bangkok and Hong Kong. In fact, if you're traveling from Europe or America and you want to sidestep Bali and Jakarta, it's often a good idea to make Singapore or KL your long-haul destination, and then book the final legs into and out of Indonesia with a budget airline.

Above A ride in a rickety outrigger might be the only way to get around in remote places like Biak off Papua.

Below AirAsia and other budget airlines have made getting around Indonesia a lot easier—and cheaper!

Below It doesn't rain all day, even at the height of the wet season, and you'll still catch a good few clear skies and fiery sunsets.

When to Travel

Peak tourist season in Indonesia is the northern summer—especially July and August. This also happens to be the best time weather-wise in this monsoonal nation, being the height of the dry season, which extends roughly from late April until October (except in northern Maluku, where everything is back to front). The wettest part of the rainy season is generally between December and February, but there's no reason to avoid Indonesia at this time—unless you're here specifically for the diving, the surfing, or the mountain climbing. It doesn't rain all day, and in any case, there's a certain thrill in the sound-and-light show of a tropical thunderstorm!

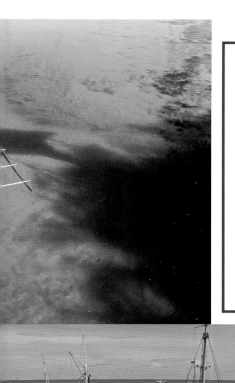

Online Planning

Indohoy We met the women behind Indohoy back in Chapter Five. They've got loads of great information, and an infectious sense of enthusiasm. www.indohoy.com

Discover Your Indonesia Firsta of Discover Your Indonesia is on a one-woman blogging mission to encourage both fellow Indonesians and foreigners to explore her homeland. www.discoveryourindonesia.com

East Indonesia I don't know how he does it, but Hungarian travel-maniac Laszlo Wagner has somehow managed to get to virtually every nook and cranny in eastern Indonesia. His website is a particularly good starting point for reading up about Maluku and Papua, places with notably thin coverage in most guidebooks. www.east-indonesia.info

Yogyes Started by a gang of local enthusiasts, Yogyes has morphed into a full-blown travel portal for all things Yogyakarta-related. There's some particularly good stuff on activities in the countryside around the city. www.yogyes.com

Right Lumbering vehicle ferries are still the mainstay of inter-island travel, with space for passengers on the upper decks.

BY BOAT, BUS, BECAK AND AIRPLANE!

The budget airline boom within Indonesian airspace has created radical new possibilities. When air travel was restricted to a couple of rickety state-owned operators charging sky-high prices, if you wanted to get to Maluku or Nusa Tenggara you were probably looking at a series of very long boat and bus trips. But now there are hundreds of very modestly priced flights to all corners of the country. Medan, Jakarta, Surabaya, Bali, and Makassar are the biggest hubs, but there are also links to every other city of any significance. In recent years there's also been a marked improvement in air services to smaller outposts, served by smaller aircraft, with Nusa

Indonesia has a few distinctive modes of transport all of its own. The becak (above) was once the mainstay of urban travel. It's the Indonesian incarnation of the pedicab; it's been around since the colonial era, and you'll still find it in the suburbs of many cities. Jakarta, meanwhile, is home to the bajaj (below), the local version of the tuk-tuk.

Tenggara and Maluku in particularly starting to unlock their doors for quick trips.

Of course, you're not going to get away without at least some travel over land and sea. The land transport infrastructure in Java is solid by the standards of the region, with a well-maintained rail network and reasonably speedy express trains linking Jakarta with all the other big cities. Intercity roads are decent too, plied by modern coaches. In Bali, however, public transport is pretty limited—almost everyone is driving themselves, or, in the case of overseas visitors, using organized tourist shuttle minibuses. Once you're out into the further reaches of the country the roads tend to get a bit rougher, and reclining seats and air-conditioning turn into a fantasy.

When it comes to boats, there are still vehicle ferry operations stitching Sumatra, Java, Bali, and Lombok together, an infinity of little local boats

As pre-booked shared taxis and air-conditioned coaches take over intercity transport, the bone-shaking old-style bus complete with proverbial chickens is slowly heading for the junkyard of history. There are still a few rough rides to be had in the remoter provinces though...

If you've got deep pockets you can travel in comfort and style in many parts of Indonesia, from luxury live-aboard cruises through Komodo **(above)** to high-end seaside hideaways in Bali **(right)**.

chugging to and from small offshore islands, and pioneering passenger ships plying the wilder spaces of Maluku. But when it comes to sea links between big cities, the budget airlines have more or less replaced them. You can still get from Kalimantan and Sulawesi to Java by boat, but you might end up waiting days or weeks for a departure, and then paying just as much as you would for an air ticket. If you're determined to sample some traditional transport, maybe the best option is to forget the long-haul ferries, and simply hop aboard a becak—an old-fashioned pedicab—for a quick rattle around Yogyakarta or any other Central or East Java city!

A PLACE TO CRASH

Accommodation in Indonesia used to be a luxurious resort in Bali or a plush but soulless business hotel in a big city if your wallet was fat, and an old-school losmen, a traditional budget guesthouse, if you were counting your

pennies—which I pretty much always am! If you're on a budget and exploring small towns and remote islands away from the main travel circuits, chances are you will still end up in those traditional places. They don't, by any means, have to be bad, though they sometimes are—think a slimy, cold-water bathroom with mosquito larvae in the mandi tank and a dust-furred fan beating slow and wonky circles over a sagging mattress with gray sheets, and a cup of lukewarm coffee and a stale chocolate-filled bread roll for breakfast.

But back in the cities, and especially in Java, the fact that local hipsters have got into the whole traveling thing has given the budget accommodation scene a new

edge. In Jakarta, there are now a whole bunch of classy capsule hostels. Also, on the fringes of the local backpacking community, Indonesians signed up for the whole Couchsurfing thing at an early stage, and there are loads of people, especially in the capital but in most other cities too, who have made a hobby of taking in houseguests. Unsurprisingly, this can, if it works out well, be one of the very best ways to tap straight into the main vein of real life in Indonesia. Airbnb has also taken off in Indonesia. You're surprised? This is Indonesia, and these things are Internet-based—they heard about them before you did!

Getting on the Road with Go-Jek

In an Internet-savvy nation like Indonesia, the idea of an interface between smartphone technology and transport was always likely to catch on. In 2015 a new mobile app was launched in Jakarta that let users order a pick-up by *ojek* (motorbike taxi). They called the app, rather brilliantly, GO-JEK. It caught on super-fast, and you can now digitally hail either a motorbike taxi or a car via the app in most major Indonesian cities for a fixed price. The Malaysia-based Grab app also offers a similar service in many parts of Indonesia. Both are cheaper and much less hassle than traditional taxis.

MAKING PLANS

I've still got a shelf full of old Indonesia guidebooks from back in the day; battered bibles with creased covers and dog-eared pages that have survived many a bone-shaking bus ride. There's the final edition of the legendary *Indonesia Handbook* from Moon Publications, a truly travel-worn copy of the 1998 Footprint guide, the lavishly illustrated island-by-island Periplus Adventure Guides (still some of the finest books for background detail if you can track down secondhand copies), and whole solar systems of Lonely Planets. There's still nothing to beat a good guidebook for getting an overview of travel possibilities in a country, but my collected vintage titles look increasingly like relics from another epoch.

These days there's still good coverage of Bali from mainstream guidebook publishers, but when it comes to the rest of Indonesia the commercially published coverage has thinned markedly—which doesn't make much sense, given that so much more of the country is now easily accessible to travelers. Ultimately, what you should always keep in mind is that what's covered in any traditional guidebook is only a fraction of what's actually out there. A case in point: Belitung, an island as big as Bali with gorgeous granite-backed beaches,

Old guidebooks from the 1990s are still a pretty good resource for background detail—and the price listings let you know just how cheap Indonesian travel once was!

a firm favorite with young travelers from Jakarta and with a burgeoning guesthouse and hotel market to serve them. Does it get a single mention in any major recently published English-language guidebook? It does not...

Happily, the coalescence of the local backpacking trend and Indonesia's Internet mania means that there's an army of digital travel writers out there furiously making up the deficit. And while many of the local backpacker blogs and travel websites publish in Indonesian, there are plenty in English too, labors of love for locals enthusiastic about sharing the attractions of their homeland with the outside world. These days the best way to make travel plans for Indonesia is often simply to look at the map, let your eye fall on any

VISAS

For years regular travelers and tourist industry leaders have been rolling their eyes at Indonesia's visa rules. They flip, they flop, they flap, and by the time a guideline appears in print, chances are some meddler in the immigration department will already have changed it. Last time I checked, citizens of ASEAN nations could usually get into Indonesia for a month without a visa, while most Europeans, North Americans, Antipodeans, and Northeast Asians could get a 30-day visa on arrival for a fee, extendable once for a further 30 days; or a non-extendable 30-day free entry stamp. If you wanted to stay longer, your best bet was to get a two-month visa in advance, which you could then extend, in theory up to four times, 30 days at a time. But please don't take my word for any of that! They're probably changing things even as we speak!

particularly tantalizing spot, grab your smartphone, and thumb the place name into Google—chances are some local adventurer will have blogged about it.

Up in the Air

I'm a nervous flyer, and Indonesia has an air safety record fit to have even the most unflappable air traveler worriedly eyeing the emergency exit. Things really came to a head after the initial bout of deregulation at the start of this century, and the subsequent free-for-all rush of low-cost airline startups—some of which, it turned out, were more concerned about getting sexy uniforms for their stewardesses than checking the nuts and bolts on their third-hand 737s. After a series of catastrophes in 2007—most notably involving the now mercifully defunct Adam Air—the European Union tossed the entire Indonesian aviation industry into its blacklist sin bin. Since then, though, things have improved considerably. The Mad Max approach to aircraft maintenance seems to mainly be a thing of the past, and those domestic airlines that survived the turbulence have mostly traded their resprayed relics for all-new fleets. Ticket costs have crept up too, under official pressure to take safety seriously, but that's surely a small price to pay. Some operators are still blacklisted by the EU, but on the whole even I can just about manage to keep my nerves under control when I take to the Indonesian skies these days!

Published by Tuttle Publishing, an imprint of Periplus Editions (HK) Ltd

www.tuttlepublishing.com

Library of Congress Cataloging-in-Publication Data

Names: Hannigan, Tim, author.
Title: A geek in Indonesia : discover the land of Balinese healers, komodo dragons and dangdut / by Tim Hannigan.
Description: First edition. | Tokyo : Tuttle Publishing, 2018.
Identifiers: LCCN 2016045866 | ISBN 9780804847100 (pbk.)
Subjects: LCSH: Indonesia--Guidebooks. | Indonesia--Social life and customs.
Classification: LCC DS614 .H36 2018 | DDC 915.9804/43--dc23 LC record available at https://lccn.loc.gov/2016045866

ISBN: 978-0-8048-4710-0

Distributed by

North America, Latin America & Europe
Tuttle Publishing
364 Innovation Drive,
North Clarendon
VT 05759-9436 U.S.A.
Tel: 1 (802) 773-8930
Fax: 1 (802) 773-6993
info@tuttlepublishing.com
www.tuttlepublishing.com

Asia Pacific
Berkeley Books Pte. Ltd.
61 Tai Seng Avenue, #02-12
Singapore 534167
Tel: (65) 6280-1330
Fax: (65) 6280-6290
inquiries@periplus.com.sg
www.periplus.com

22 21 20 19 18
5 4 3 2 1

Printed in China
1711RR

ABOUT TUTTLE:
BOOKS TO SPAN THE EAST AND WEST

Our core mission at Tuttle Publishing is to create books which bring people together one page at a time. Tuttle was founded in 1832 in the small New England town of Rutland, Vermont (USA). Our fundamental values remain as strong today as they were then—to publish best-in-class books informing the English-speaking world about the countries and peoples of Asia. The world has become a smaller place today and Asia's economic, cultural and political influence has expanded, yet the need for meaningful dialogue and information about this diverse region has never been greater. Since 1948, Tuttle has been a leader in publishing books on the cultures, arts, cuisines, languages and literatures of Asia. Our authors and photographers have won numerous awards and Tuttle has published thousands of books on subjects ranging from martial arts to paper crafts. We welcome you to explore the wealth of information available on Asia at **www.tuttlepublishing.com**